GET OFF THE
HAMSTER WHEEL

**The New Moon Method to
Reset, Reboot, and Replant**

ADRIAN S. WINDSOR, PH.D.

ISBN: 978-0-9892907-6-0

Publisher

McGregor Wood LLC
14252 Culver Dr. #352A
Irvine, CA 92604
www.adrianwindsor.com

Printed in the United States of America

CONTENTS

PREFACE...V

INTRODUCTION..1

PART 1: LIFE'S SENTENCE....................................17

    THE SENTENCE...19

    MAKING ENDS MEET...29

    INHERENT EVIL..41

    LIMITS: LIVING SOMEONE ELSE'S IDEA.........53

    TOO EASY: THE OXEN AND THE EAGLE·.........65

PART 2: A CONCEPTUAL FRAMEWORK.............77

    WE ARE ALL ASTRONAUTS..............................79

    TRIAL AND ERROR...89

    THE METAPHYSICAL CONTEXT.......................99

PART 3: RESET...105

    NO MISTAKES:...107
    Only Opportunities to Discover the Truth

    PIANO TOPS...123

PART 4 REBOOT..143

    BIG PICTURE..145

    TRUE WEALTH..165

PART 5: REPLANT..185

    LEVERAGE..187

    SYNERGY..209

    BE A GREAT PIRATE..235

CONCLUSION..261

APPENDIX..265

ACKNOWLEDGEMENTS..281

REFERENCE NOTES..285

BIBLIOGRAPHY..293

PREFACE

My grandfather was a Michigan garden farmer who grew amazing crops on his 300 acres of dark, black, rich muck soil on his farm between Saline and Clinton, Michigan. As a child, I just took the diversity for granted: corn, cucumbers, tomatoes, watermelons, cantaloupe, strawberries, cauliflower, broccoli, kohlrabi, potatoes, beets, turnips, parsnips. He imported grapes from Italy and made his own wine. His hobby was growing flowers – delphinium, foxgloves, Canterbury bells, larkspur – wonderful, healthy perennials.

I loved to go with him to the Detroit Farmer's Market on Third Street. Each night during the summer, he and my grandmother would get into the Rio truck at 11:00 p.m. to make the drive to Detroit. If I were lucky, I would get to ride in the back of the truck on top of the load. This was long before child safety or seat belts. My father never liked for me to go with them. Grandpa had lost one arm in a combine, and he steered the truck with one hand and his stump. Fifteen minutes of sleep for him was the equivalent of two hours for someone else. But my father was always afraid he might fall asleep at the wheel.

Halfway there, he would stop the truck and we would go into the restaurant for coffee and a snack. Then we would get back into the truck and proceed to market. About 3:00 a.m., the Jewish merchants would bang on his truck cab door, where he and my grandma were taking a snooze. They would call out, "Cully, Cully." My grandfather's name was Columbach Happel. He was German and Austrian.

My grandfather would get out of the truck and start to negotiate. They would haggle and haggle. Grandpa and the Jews were from the same part of the world, and I always knew he was part Jewish. They spoke the same language. If Grandpa got the right price, he would sell the whole load, and we would go unload it at the store and go to breakfast. I hated when that happened. There went all of our fun.

When he didn't get the right price, then we would go to breakfast, and on to the Farmer's market to retail the load. Grandpa was so proud that I could make change when I was only four. If any woman attempted to peel down an ear of corn, he would command: "Unhand my corn. I have the best corn in the market. You either buy it as it is, or go somewhere else." He knew each woman who had bought flowers from him by first name, and they would line up to tell him about yellow leaves or pests or fertilizer issues.

The title of this book comes from my experience with my grandfather. He farmed by the book, *The Farmer's Almanac*. He gauged every activity by the sign of the moon. For crops that produced fruit below the ground – potatoes, beets, turnips, parsnips – he planted when the moon was full. For crops that produced fruit above the ground out into the light, he planted when the moon was new – strawberries, melons, cucumbers, tomatoes, corn, cabbage, lettuce, kohlirabi.

The fruit of the "New Moon" was not only my favorite, but also it had a cheerfulness to its nature. You did not store "New Moon" produce in dark, damp, smelly fruit cellars. You either ate it or canned it at its peak. Nothing ever tasted better than a tomato on the vine warmed by the sun or a hunk of the watermelon that someone just happened to drop in the field. It is applicable to our life.

The new moon is richly metaphoric for determining when to plant and what to plant if we want to grow our life. New moons are a blank page upon which to speak our dreams out loud and to state our intent. When we enter the new moon, the moon is completely dark. During this phase, the moon is hidden from sight due to the earth's position between the sun and the moon: The Dark of the Moon. No sunlight is reflected back down to us from the moon's surface. This is a time to let go, to banish anything that does not serve us.

This can be a little frightening, because when we let go, there is uncertainty. It has a void and empty quality. But unless we let go, we cannot allow the "new" to flow into our lives. This is the moment when the old passes away and the new is not here yet. This is when we send out our prayers, wishes, and desires to the universe, even though we cannot yet see to plant them. Letting go of what no longer serves us while trusting is a cleansing act, an act of pure faith that the light will return.

It is typical human behavior to be hamsters on a wheel, going around and around, doing the same thing over and over, and as so often observed, expecting different results. Getting off that wheel is a wrenching experience, but we can do it. I was recently grinding coffee at our local Costco when the machine stopped. I looked around for someone to assist me, and no one was in sight   Then I thought, "There must be a reset button." And yes, there at the bottom of the machine was a tiny white button. I pressed it, and the machine took off again. We forget there is a reset button. This was brought home to me in a recent conversation with an IT person. He said that whenever anyone comes to him with a problem, the first thing he says is, "Reboot!" That usually works. He doesn't have to do another thing. Instead of reset and reboot, how often do we repeat, rehash, regret the story we are telling about ourselves.

So, reset, reboot, then what? If we don't plant something different, select the right seed for the desired fruit, we will continue to reap what we have sown before. We become so mired in habit, so accustomed to striving to fulfill the expectations other people have about us that we forget who we are, who we are meant to be. As R. Buckminster Fuller once observed about his new "discoveries," they had a musty smell, as if they had been there all along, just waiting to be uncovered. I truly believe that we come into this world as a spark ready to be fanned into flame, only too often to be extinguished.

You will find a series of exercises in the "Appendix" of this book. If you choose to do them, you will have the opportunity to "inventory" your past and your present, to determine what you might wish to reset and reboot. It will facilitate the release of the Dark Side of the Moon and will prepare you to replant the seeds of attitudes, behaviors, and practices to empower you to grow your life.

INTRODUCTION

Life on the front porch

WHEN I WAS a child growing up in a small Michigan town, I lived on Elm Street. It was a street lined with maple trees, not elm trees. The houses had front porches, and they represented a way of life. In the evening, from early spring through autumn when it got too cold, we would gather on the front porch. Those porches would be equipped in a variety of ways. Our first house at 612 Elm Street had a porch swing, and I spent long summer afternoons reading and swinging on that porch. When we moved to 604 Elm Street, the porch was screened in. That meant that we could enjoy the evening breeze mosquito-free, and even have a lamp for reading because we didn't need to worry about the light attracting insects. Most porches had a glider. A glider is a sofa that sways back and forth, situated firmly on the surface of the porch, not suspended like a swing. Sometimes people had hammocks on their porches, but the problem with a hammock was that it could only accommodate one person.

The front porch represented a way of life. Because it was a front porch, it faced the street and the sidewalk. The houses on both sides of the street thus faced each other. We could look into the windows of our neighbors, and they could look into ours. We always knew who was on the porch and who was in the house, who was home and who wasn't. There was constant movement, house to house and porch to porch. We knew what the neighbors were having for supper, we knew when they were fighting, and we even knew what they were fighting about. We knew that some people preferred to "keep to themselves," and we knew that some people were "nosey." But we really knew that if anyone needed help, all they had to do was ask. When we entered each other's houses, that is across the front porch and into the front door, we would yell, "You hoo! Is anybody home?" Of course, we knew already.

One big chat room

In today's way of looking at the world, one would say we were networked, organized as one big chat room. We moved outward, block by block, but our own block was our center, and we knew it. We had tolerance for each other's idiosyncrasies and differences; it was forced upon us in order to live together. We learned to speak up when the neighbor's kids did something wrong; and we learned quickly that sooner or later, usually sooner, we would get "told on" if we wandered outside the mark. That mark was clearly defined, not by written words but by neighborhood practice. In other words, the ethical standards and the moral values were firm. No one seemed to think very much about what they had or didn't have. Some of the neighbors got a new car every other year. And some of the neighbors just kept their old cars. Some things the neighbors did were your business, and some things were none of your business. Most of the time we knew the difference. When we got too nosey, we might get told, "It's none of your business."

When life revolved around the front porch, especially in summer, there was a sense of peace and prosperity. The father would come home from work, have supper, maybe work in the yard, and then go sit on the front porch. Some mothers worked, too; but as soon as the chores were done, they would come out on the porch. The Armstrongs, who were Catholic and had lots of kids, worked as a team from home. They "hung wallpaper." It would be not the right thing to do to ask anyone but the Armstrongs to hang your wallpaper; they had so many kids and they worked so hard. The Hansons had a beer tavern, so Mr. Hanson worked late. It was ok for the Hansons to be in the beer business, because they were German and Germans drink beer. Actually, the whole neighborhood was called German Hill because so many of the neighbors were German.

The front porch tolerance

As kids, we played in the street and moved back and forth to each other's porches. At 6:15 we would gather on the steps of one of our porches to watch the nuns walk from Sienna Heights College to St. Joseph's Church. It was a mystery what they had under their black and white habits. My father said they shaved their heads. When we were told to come in, that meant to come home to our own porch. We might still be carrying on a conversation with the kids next door, just porch to porch instead of hip to haunch. Sometimes we played kick the can, sometimes hide and seek, sometimes tag, sometimes school, and sometimes doctor. We were all better at some things than at others, and we accepted deficiency as a given. Harold C., for instance, "wasn't all there," so he could play hide and seek, but he couldn't play school. It wasn't a good idea to play doctor with Walter A. in the bushes because he conducted physical examination in such detail.

I remember when my cousin, Wanda, moved out of town, and I went there to baby sit. The houses were all in a row, but none had a front porch. Instead, there was a garage door facing the street. All of the houses looked exactly alike. Her children were supposed to play only in the back yard, and they weren't allowed on the street. In the evening what they really liked to do was just watch television. It made it easy to baby sit. They had a concrete patio in the back, but it wasn't screened in, and they didn't go out there too often. Their back yard was separated from the neighbors on both sides by a fence, and each family kept to itself. Wanda liked it better that way because she didn't have the neighbors bothering her. She was too busy for that. She was a nurse.

Our houses and our porches metaphorically express our orientation not only to our world, but also to our experiences. R. Buckminster Fuller, the inventor of the geodesic dome, cared about houses. Much of his life work was spent trying to figure out how to house all of humanity. Since the tools I offer here to reset, reboot, and replant evolved from concepts explored in

4

his *Operating Manual for Spaceship Earth*, there is an underlying assumption that the planet is our house, fully exposed and fully networked within Universe. Life lived from the garage door symbolizes the rat race, separation and anxiety: "making ends meet." Life lived from the front porch is more tranquil, peaceful, harmonious, under beneficent control. I believe we can live again from the front porch.

Return to leisure and peace

This spaceship we're riding on is really quite small, and we can't avoid acknowledging we inhabitant the same house. The Internet shrinks its size a little more every day. It is important that we mind each other's business, that we be our brother's keepers, that we know the rules, that we take advantage of shared resources, that we be tolerant of each others' differences, that we each develop our true wealth, and that we use every tool available to do it.

Beware when the great God lets loose a thinker on this planet. Then all things are at risk. It is as when a conflagration has broken out in a great city, and no man knows what is safe, or where it will end. There is not a piece of science but its flank may be turned to-morrow; there is not any literary reputation, not the so-called eternal names of fame that may not be revised and condemned. The very hopes of man, the thoughts of his heart, the religion of nations, the manners and morals of mankind are all at the mercy of a new generalization. Generalization is always a

new influx of the divinity into the mind. Hence the thrill
that attends it.

Emerson, "Circles"[1]

Housing for humanity

In the early eighties I was led to make a public commitment to bring the ideas of R. Buckminster Fuller to the public.
Although Fuller is best known as the inventor of the geodesic
dome, as one reviews his lifetime of invention, it is apparent
that the dome was the last of many designs he created out of his
compassionate concern for housing humanity. He wanted to
produce portable houses that could be dropped into the most
remote deserts, the deepest forests, and the highest mountains.
His intention was to use these houses domestically, but in fact
the military probably took the greatest advantage of his designs.

The geodesic dome is definitely Fuller's most important
invention. In fact, he is known so much for this invention
that when, in 1996, three chemists, Harold Kroto of England's
University of Sussex, and Richard Smalley and Robert Curl of
Rice University in Houston, were awarded the Nobel Peace
Prize for the discovery of a molecule shaped like a geodesic
dome, they named it after him. They called the molecules,
formed in the crystal residue that results from mixing helium
with the carbon vapor produced by zapping graphite with a
laser beam, "buckminsterfullerenes," shortened to "buckyballs."
These molecules, composed of 60 carbon atoms, have hollow
interiors that make them extremely valuable for conduction of
electricity and drug delivery systems.

The commitment

My commitment to promote Fuller's teaching was made during a seminar with the stated purpose of empowering people to be more effective in their lives. Fuller's ideas were at the core of this seminar, especially the concepts of leverage and synergy. Both words now have such common occurrence in our everyday speech that it seems amazing that groups of knowledgeable and essentially well-educated people would come together to be introduced to these ideas as fresh and vital. Yet here I am writing about them again in a way that I think will be meaningful to you to help you *reset, reboot,* and *replant.* Certainly, since speaking intent attracts the flow of events and resources to make ideas reality, I must regard it as a natural evolution from Fuller's inspiration that this book has taken form.

Always sales

I am a business woman, a real estate broker and the head of a privately held corporation, yet by education and professional training, I am also an educator. Although I left formal *academia*, I am still teaching and will probably always be teaching in whatever I do. At the heart of the experience is the relationship between teacher and student, that cottage industry where it all began, with the itinerant teacher sharing the word with anyone who would listen, from Socrates onward. In formal *academia*, as frequently happens with good teachers, I found myself "elevated" to administration, not realizing that in entering bureaucracy, I was abandoning my essential nature, that of the entrepreneur.

The teacher in the classroom is an entrepreneur, taking her product to market, so to speak, and convincing the buyer that life without it will not really be worth living. I tell my students today that "Life is sales!" Selling Homer, Sophocles and Aeschyulus to undergraduates at 8:00 a.m., in retrospect, was actually a bigger and more momentous challenge than selling a multi-million dollar house or a forty million dollar office building. It was only after leaving *academia*, entering business, and then re-entering the classroom, that I thoroughly understood my role in that position of leadership, not as one who keeps and dispenses information and gives grades to punish and reward, but rather as one who offers an opportunity for transformation. It seemed appropriate, as my business makes it increasingly difficult to set time aside for teaching, that I now put my teaching into book form, actually "practicing what I preach": leverage.

Fuller and Emerson

More than a decade and a half after I left my academic profession at Colorado Women's College and the University of Colorado at Boulder, I met the Dean at Coastline Community College, a campus without walls that serves more adults and immigrants than traditional-aged students. He invited me to come and teach a writing course. I agreed to accept on the condition that I be able to select the texts that would generate the subject matter of the students' writing. My choice was Fuller's *Operating Manual for Spaceship Earth* and Emerson's *Essays*, moving from the planet to the inner self, with the purpose to provide tools to make them more effective in whatever they undertake in life.

Some of these tools are drawn from the concepts that underlie Fuller's *Operating Manual for Spaceship Earth*.[2] The manual, he contends, we have created and developed over the history of mankind through our discovery of how our planet operates, through the evolution of our "know how." With Emerson's inspiration, we discover that each of us has a unique ability, a special calling, an "inner genius," a talent waiting to be acknowledged and tapped. This is that spark at birth, often extinguished, likely to have a musty smell when we finally rediscover it. Emerson expresses my function as a teacher in the concluding words of his essay, "Experience": "The transformation of genius into practical power." [3]

Perfect Universe: Perfect Intelligence

The thesis of *Operating Manual for Spaceship Earth* is that the planet came without an operating manual allowing human beings who reside here to figure out the way it works. It works perfectly, indeed, has always worked perfectly. The only thing that changes is our understanding. Here in the twenty-first century, our knowledge is growing exponentially, and revisions in our understanding are coming so quickly we can hardly absorb them. Fuller assumes a perfect intelligence created this perfectly operating planet, and he presents the concepts and principles that inform that operation. He calls this "livingry" and ardently challenges us to use these concepts and principles to get our share of the natural abundance.

Past ideas and present belief
Climate of opinion

We all bring to wherever we are whatever we have come to *believe* based on our personal experience. I picked up ideas on the front porch that have been with me most of my life, some useful, some destructive, some limiting. Since effective change can only take place when we know how we got to *believe* what we *believe*, we will begin with an examination of the belief system many of us carry around, created by a combination of climate of opinion and race consciousness. When I use the term "climate of opinion," I am referring to the ideas integrated into our thinking because of: things our parents have told us; things our teachers, relatives, and friends say or do; things we read in mass publications such as newspapers and the grocery story check-out line magazines; and things the media chooses to stress on television and the radio. Other people's "importances" affect our world view and skew our vision.

Race consciousness

When I use the term "race consciousness," I am adopting but re-phrasing the terminology of Ernest Holmes who wrote of "race suggestion."[4] This was his catch-all term for what we inherit in our belief system from the beginning of man, our prejudices, our attitudes, our fears. It is an envelope of life with origins so deep in our psyche, our "collective unconscious," as defined by Karl Jung, it often emerges with clarity only in our dreams because it can be so frightening. It may go back to our cave man origins when wind or lightening or thunder threatened our existence. It may have been expressed in philosophy, in religion, in poetry, and so penetrated our thinking it would never occur to us to think otherwise.

Level playing field

As I examine climate of opinion and race consciousness, my intent is not to pass judgment, but to be aware. As we know and accept the belief systems that have formed, nurtured, and sustained us, they lose their power. This is what the art critic Roger Fry called the "aesthetic experience," the moment when the artist looks at nature and sees it whole so that each of the elements loses its individual importance, and he then is able to paint the canvas as God has painted it, in its entirety. As we release the beliefs or attitudes that control us, hold us back or direct us to self-sabotage, we are more free to take advantage of the tools that Universe has provided for us so plentifully, to give metaphysical application to the physical concepts that make things run, to accept cause and effect and to harness action and reaction positively in our life.

My hamster wheel

Since I cannot speak for you, I will speak for myself. During those long summer days and evenings on the front porch, I collected and stashed away the climate of opinion and race consciousness I affectionately call my "hamster wheel." My intent is not so much to beat myself up in public, as it is to just let you know I've carried around my fair share of garbage, have dumped some, and am working at dumping the rest. You may have some of mine, and I'm sure you have some of your own. These beliefs and attitudes held me in bondage:

A sample list of these beliefs and attitudes

My hamster wheel picked up on the porch:

* We are living a life sentence.
* Life is a struggle to make ends meet.
* Man is inherently sinful and evil.
* We all have our limits.
* Anything easy isn't worth doing.
* An open path is out of control.
* We are not whole unless we have a mate.
* God keeps score.
* Success and failure are pure luck.

My touchstones

Once we've examined what is keeping us on the wheel, we'll be ready to examine the creation of a perfect mind in action, the work of Universe, the masterpiece of a freely giving God. The message is grounded in optimism, confirming the enormous capacity of the human mind and spirit to solve every problem. Throughout this book I have drawn upon my personal touchstones from fiction and poetry, and I have freely used the experiences of my students and myself as illustration and demonstration. We teach what we need to learn. In teaching my students, I have been confirming my faith that there is a perfect pattern for our experience; that human beings, though frail, susceptible, selfish, and greedy, have an enormous resilience and intuitive impulse toward good; that we can re-invent ourselves and our life in accordance with our chosen vision; that Universe, God, has provided all the tools we need and is just waiting for us to wake up and pay attention.

Seven concepts: seven tools to get off the hamster wheel

We will deal with seven concepts derived and distilled from Fuller: No Mistakes: Only Opportunities to Discover the Truth, Piano Tops, Big Picture, True Wealth, Leverage, Synergy, and Great Pirate. You are invited to participate at your chosen level in self-assessment and analysis to envision your perfect life, to determine the steps you will take, and to integrate beneficial attitudes and practices.   You will find exercises in the "Appendix" to facilitate the process.

If you choose to follow the complete path, to embrace the New Moon Method, you will:

RESET

* Discard irrelevancies, Mistakes, and greet challenges proactively.
* Let go of outmoded behavior patterns, Piano Tops.

REBOOT

* Envision your Big Picture and take command of your navigational path
* Tap into your True Wealth and accept abundance.

REPLANT

* Use Leverage to do more with less.
* Create Synergy in your families, your relationships, your work.
* Become a Great Pirate and take sovereignty over your life.

YOU WILL GET OFF THE HAMSTER WHEEL.

I'm Nobody! Who are you?
Are you –Nobody—too?
Then there's a pair of us!
Don't tell! They'd banish us—you know!

How dreary—to be—somebody!
How pubic—like a Frog—
To tell your name—the livelong day—
To an admiring Bog.
    Emily Dickinson, 1861

From *Sailing to Byzantium*
    An Aged man is but a paltry thing,
    A tattered coat upon a stick, unless
    Soul clap its hands and sing,
    and louder sing
    For every tatter in its mortal dress.
        W. B. Yeats, 1926

From *The Road Not Taken*
    I shall be telling this with a sigh
    Somewhere ages and ages hence:
    Two roads diverged in a wood, and I—
    I took the one less traveled by,
    And that has made all the difference.
        Robert Frost, 1916

From *Sympathy*
    I know why the caged bird sings, ah me,
    When his wing is bruised and his bosom sore,--
    When he beat his bars and he would be free;
    It is not a carol of joy or glee
    But a prayer that he sends from his heart's deep core,
    But a plea, that upward to Heaven he fling—
    I know why the caged bird sings.
        Paul Laurence Dunbar, 1899

PART 1: LIFE'S SENTENCE

* We all accepted a life sentence, derived from our parents, race consciousness and climate of opinion. It binds us to the hamster wheel.

* We aren't stuck with the sentence.

* As masters of our thoughts and directors of our actions, we can choose the *who, what, when, where* and *how* of our life.

No man can learn what he has not preparation for learning, however near to his eyes is the object.... God screens us evermore from premature ideas. Our eyes are holden that we cannot see things that stare us in the face, until the hour arrives when the mind is ripened; then we behold them, and the time when we saw them not is like a dream.

Emerson, "Spiritual Laws" [1]

THE SENTENCE

The cat in the bag

I OFTEN USE the "cat in a bag" analogy to describe the writing process and the writer's relationship to sentences. Once an idea is articulated by symbols, once the words are on paper, a commitment is made. No matter how empty of content, no matter how confused the presentation of the ideas, no matter how limited the vocabulary, no matter how poorly constructed the syntax, the sentence exists; and once written, the writer is determined to deal with it in its present form. He may punch, pull, jab, squeeze, attack, wrench, wiggle, and squiggle, but the basic sentence is still there. The sentence is like a cat caught in a burlap sack, trying to escape, unable to get out, trapped by the context. You are that writer, stuck with the sentence, or so it seems. The only solution, the best solution, is to throw the sentence out and start over; but because the sentence *is*, you continue to wrestle with it. Analogous to the cat, the more the cat struggles the more the claws are immobilized. It doesn't have to be that way. Guess what? You are that writer. It's your sentence. You wrote it; you can get rid of it; you can start over. It's only a sentence. This is such a metaphor for life. We desire to deal with and fix the status quo, no matter how rotten it is. We truly believe we are stuck with the sentence. We are stuck on the hamster wheel.

Death by drowning

Kafka's short story, "The Judgment,"[2] is about a father, a son, and a sentence.

Kafka's works, like the works of all great writers, are about his own unresolved issues, the insecure young man, dissatisfied with his accomplishments because nothing he does is quite good enough, trapped by circumstances and dominated by the powerful, overbearing, unsympathetic and judgmental father. In "The Judgment," the mother has been dead for two years, and the father and son, Georg, are sharing the same house and working together in the business. Since the mother's death, Georg has begun to succeed in the business, and he has even become engaged to be married. On a Sunday morning he enters the father's part of the house where he is sitting in darkness. Georg looks at him and thinks, "My father is still a giant of a man." Quite the contrary. The father is old, physically weak, and physically powerless. Georg puts him to bed, covers him up.

As the conversation between the father and son progresses, as they begin to disagree, we come to understand that the son is a split personality, torn apart. He knows he is succeeding, but no matter what he accomplishes, he will never meet his father's expectations, his father's image of what his son should be. The father rises up out of the bed, says to Georg, "I sentence you now to death by drowning." Georg opens the door, rushes down the stairs and across the street to the bridge. As he jumps in the water, he speaks his final lie, "Dear parents, I have always loved you, all the same."

A "gigantic insect"

In another of Kafka's works, "The Metamorphosis,"[3] the hero, a traveling salesman, hates his job, his employer, and his life. Burdened by the chore of supporting his parents and sister, he awakens one morning and discovers he's a bug: "As Gregor Samsa awoke one morning from uneasy dreams he found himself transformed in his bed into a gigantic insect." As the story unfolds, we see that this is his sentence, imposed upon him by the way he sees himself: Enslaved to his company; enslaved to his parents and the debt they incurred; accused by his employer of laziness, neglect, possible theft; surrounded by scoundrels and at the mercy of circumstances. By becoming a bug, a giant cockroach, no less, he is escaping from his sentence in life. As a bug he no longer has to go to work, no longer has to do his parents' bidding, no longer has to bow and scrape, to be a machine for other people.

The dung beetle trashed

The family decides that they must "get rid of the old dung beetle;" even his sister, who has treated him with the most kindness, announces he must go: "I won't utter my brother's name in the presence of this creature, and so all I say is we must try to get rid of it." Gregor, who had "not the slightest intention of frightening anyone far less his sister," retreats and his sister slams, bolts, and locks the door behind him, startling him so much that "his little legs gave beneath him." As Gregor breathes his last breath, "He thought of his family with tenderness and love. The decision that he must disappear was one that he held to even more strongly than his sister, if that were possible." The charwoman finds him the next day: "Indeed, Gregor's body was completely flat and dry, as could only now be seen when it was no longer supported by legs and nothing prevented one from looking closely at it." The father, mother, and sister decide to sell the house, to move into a smaller place, to begin a new life. Gregor is gone and forgotten.

Sentenced

Both Georg and Gregor commit suicide. The psychologist, Theodore Reik observed through his work with clients that depression is rage against someone else turned against yourself; and suicide, likewise, is a death wish against someone near and dear, again turned against yourself. Georg is sentenced by his father, and Gregor sentences himself. In both instances, however, the sentence can only stick if the individual accepts it, owns it, acts upon it. Kafka is extreme, so if you haven't drowned or turned into a bug, take a big, deep, fresh breath. You are, however, sentenced. Someone sentenced all of us. It may be a parent, a spouse, or we ourselves.

But not stuck

We, however, are not stuck with the sentence, for we have the option of writing our own. We are at choice. We may handle our life experience like Georg, acting out someone else's orders, someone else's ideas. We may handle it like Gregor, turning ourselves into a cockroach, escaping from reality by living out a nightmare. Or we may choose to rid ourselves of the sentence and start over. The truth is we need act out the sentence only if we accept it. *We* give the sentence its power. Indeed, the very people who sentenced us usually didn't know they were doing it. They were only living out *their own* sentences.

Our Hamster Wheel

Whenever we begin to think about change, it is helpful to take an inventory of our hamster wheel. Is it based on what we perceive to be given to us? Did we write our own? Or did we write our own based on what we heard from someone or somewhere else? Whatever we perceive to be our sentence, is our sentence. For what we perceive, what we accept, we take on as our burden. Then we write it out in our own words. It is now ours to be lived out. That's why we call it baggage or our stuff. This is our baggage; this is our block; this is our sentence. I did say, however, that we are at choice. We may choose the hamster wheel, or we may choose to discard the burden and be free. We may not be able to dump all the baggage in one fell swoop; but if we know it for what it is, we may be able to set it aside for a time, if only to trip over it later on.

The baggage inventory

In my experience, just the ability to identify and to label an emotion, a fear, or a belief, takes away its power. Since I have done this for myself, although I would never claim to be totally baggage free, I am going to inventory my baggage for you in the next few chapters because I am intimately acquainted with it. It came to me from many sources: my family, the climate of opinion, race consciousness. I picked up some of it on the front porch. From these sources I wrote my own sentence.

The teachings of Fuller and Emerson have encouraged me to let the cat out of the bag, to start over, to *reset, reboot,* and *replant.* The following summary of my sentence may or may not resonate with you. You may not have all of my baggage. Good! Chances are, however, you have some of it. And you will have your own, regardless. Let me say this **was** my sentence. I use the past tense, because I hopefully have taught and written it out of myself - not a pretty journey, but a necessary one. Note that my sentence has multiple parts.

My Sentence

We must make ends meet because we are inherently evil. I grew up believing that in life, we have to make ends meet. This can only be done through struggle because we were meant to struggle. Since there actually isn't quite enough for everybody, we have to get ours. God set us up for it from the very beginning. The minute the serpent tempted Eve and together they tempted Adam to eat that apple, we were doomed. No matter how pure we may appear on the outside, inside we are evil. For those who call this sin, there's a way out with a savior. If we don't like to label this predicament as sin, and have not accepted a savior, then at the best we must see man as a social animal, creating and perpetually tangled in social problems needing resolution. Either way, we are inherently trapped. If that weren't bad enough, we have limits. It really doesn't matter who imposed those limits, because we have to deal with them ourselves.

If it's easy, it's worthless.

Because there isn't enough, because we have to struggle to make ends meet, and because we have our limits, anything that comes too easily has no value. We can only define ourselves through hard work. We may have great potential, halfway up Jacob's ladder, somewhere between the highest of heaven and the lowest of earth, but we have our place. If we rock the boat, we might land in the water and drown. It doesn't matter whether we're right or not. Isn't that the source of the term "dead right?" Who are we to presume and assume we can slide easily into first base when life was meant from the start to be an immense cat's cradle with us entangled right in the middle?

Emotional ideas rule.

These are the emotional ideas that have ruled my life. It has taken me a lifetime to realize that although my limits were set by my parents, I'm the one who gave them reality, who gave them power. I sentenced myself. As we examine these beliefs in the following chapters, one by one, some may be familiar to you. My intent is that they will fade into the woodwork under the scrutiny of the pure, bright, intellectual light, or at least, like Gregor, hide in the woodwork until they die and decay. It is possible to reverse a life sentence; it is possible to remold and remake the sentence we write for ourselves. It is possible to get off the hamster wheel, to *reset, reboot* and *replant.*

We are afraid of truth, afraid of fortune, afraid of death, and afraid of each other. Our age yields no great and perfect persons. We want men and women who shall renovate life and our social state, but we see that most natures are insolvent, cannot satisfy their own wants, have an ambition out of all proportion to their practical force and do lean and beg day and night continually.

Emerson, "Self Reliance"[1]

MAKING ENDS MEET

Thrift

IN SHAKESPEARE'S *HAMLET*, when his mother, Gertrude, marries his uncle immediately after his father's mysterious death, "most wicked speed, to post, /With such dexterity to incestuous sheets," Hamlet comments quixotically to Horatio: "Thrift, thrift, Horatio! The funeral baked meats/Did coldly furnish forth the marriage tables." I,ii, 179-81. If you thought that was a good idea, using leftovers from the funeral for the wedding banquet the next day, then you probably also add extra water to the soup to stretch it, pour milk in the pan drippings to make gravy, and make one little can of tuna fish feed four people by adding celery and boiled eggs. These are all ways of making ends meet.

Scarcity Consciousness

"Making ends meet," an old saying, comes from fear and anxiety. R. Buckminster Fuller called it the Malthus/Marx/

Darwin/Entropy consciousness.[2] This is the consciousness that tells us that the planet is running out of food for the people because there are so many of us, that the unenlightened task-masters who do the manual labor are more important than the thinkers, that only the fittest can survive in the "dog eat dog" world we live in, and that in the long run it won't matter anyway because the planet is running out of energy. This is a "doers are more important than thinkers" philosophy.

The Wired, the Kluge, and the Provincial

In an article, "The Fate of a Nation,"[3] published in the "Opinion" section of the *LA Times*, David Friedman divided our populace in the United States into three economies: the Wired, the Kluge (name taken from Rube Goldberg), and the Provincial. His categories, admittedly, are gross generalities, yet they provide a workable framework for understanding this scarcity consciousness and the prevailing climate of opinion. His thesis is that the Wired, the Bill Gates, Mark Zuckerbergs and Steve Jobs' successors will prevail and will determine the fate of the nation because they will hire more people and because the Wired hold the future.

What he observes, however, is that politics is controlled by the Kluge, comprised of: 1) the media and 2) the bureaucrats in public institutions and education. The Wired are too preoccupied in their creative and productive activity to be mired down in the slow pace of bureaucracy. The Provincial, the Tea Party and Patriot groups, dominate in rural America, among blue-collar workers, in conservative political circles. They are distrustful of the Wired, wary of technology, and challenged by change. We know the Provincial as much for what they're *against* as for what they're *for*. They are against international trade, against NAFTA, against uncontrolled immigration, against planetary initiatives, against climate change, against free choice, against U.S. involvement in NATO's military actions and, indeed, any military action where our national interest is not at stake.

Kluge fires and Provincial fears

The scarcity consciousness in the climate of opinion is acted upon, expressed and articulated by the Kluge and the Provincial. The Kluge in politics and *academia* protect the *status quo*, and the Kluge in media exploit the sensational. The power of the Kluge creates a poll-driven President, manipulated by the climate of opinion rather than by principle. The Kluge fuel the predictions of the Provincial that the fabric of our society has come unraveled and our worst fears are being realized.

The Provincials lament our jobs are being lost to nations with cheap labor, our imbalance of trade is undermining our economy, and our nation is torn apart by sex, immorality, and violence. The message that sells to them is based on fear and scarcity. We must protect what we have. We must circle up the tents to protect the American family, and we must protect our borders because there's scarcely enough for everyone, because it's a struggle in this world to "make ends meet." This thought rules many of our lives; we have given our sovereignty to it.

Up and dressed

When I was a child in Michigan, it was a major accomplishment in the morning to be up and dressed. Even though both of my parents worked, there was usually someone at home with me in the morning, a grandmother, an aunt, a baby sitter. Dressing was leisurely. Before I left for school, Happy Hank would check through the radio with his magic eye to see that the house was left neat and tidy. And then off I would go, a block and a half to school. When it rained I carried a half-broken umbrella, retrieved from a neighbor's trash on pick-up day. The children in my kindergarten class were critical of the umbrella until I told them it was a special umbrella because it was Chinese. In those days, Chinese was exotic, not cheap.

Now, half a century later, contrary to news of the booming economy, I sometimes think the Malthus/Marx/Darwin/Entropy consciousness has proven its validity. As I sit down to write this morning, there are homes all over the United States where one or two parents are arising at 4:00 a.m. to begin their day. This is what they have ahead of them: getting themselves up and dressed; getting the children up and dressed and driven to day care; making the commute to work where they will stay eight or ten or twelve hours; picking their children up from day care.

No relief in sight

The *LA Times* reports the parental strain in an article, "The Six O'Clock Scramble"[4] relating the difficulty for parents, faced with long work days, to get back to day care by 6:00 p.m., the closing time, to pick up their children. The quality of life in America, with all of our mechanical domestic appliances, has not increased along with the gross national product. Again, the *LA Times* carries a headline: "Our Culture of Efficiency Has Made Life Harder."[5] The author, Mary McNamara, observes that "'ability to multi-task a must' is now a standard job description tagline, and seminars and workshops continue to appear like toadstools after too much rain." The multi-task tagline is generally directed toward women. The more gadgets and appliances we have to help us, to make our life "easier," the more women are expected to do.

During the 2008 recession following the sub-prime mortgage fiasco, more women went to work than men. Companies could hire women for less money, offer them fewer or no benefits, and they would do the job often better than the men. The balance of power shifted in many families. The wife became the bread-winner and the husband the housekeeper. That is not really the truth. The wife still had the major burden of the home and children in addition to the job. The men sent out resumes and dealt with their depression.

The haves and the have-nots

This shift in balance exacerbated the distinction between the haves and have-nots.

The haves

On the have side, there are salaried employees who work for *avant-garde* firms who have all of the extra privileges for employees and their families: day care in the company, job sharing, maternity leave for either parent, health insurance, dental insurance, vision insurance, 401K's, and paid vacations. Facebook and Google now even offer "egg freezing" for women who have postponed child-bearing for their careers. Sheryl Sandberg, author of *Lean In*, got the company to provide up-close parking for pregnant women. Although the epitome of the "have," she understands completely, however, the mine-field most women with ambition must navigate and the challenges they face in their multiple roles.

The working hours seem to get longer and the line between the haves and the have-nots has become more distinct. In California, the 40-hour week with extra pay for overtime was a disputed legislative issue. With that settled in 2016, salaried employees can no longer be expected to work as many hours as it takes to get the job done, but the enforcement has become a playing field for lawyers.

The have-nots

On the have-not side, are the people who lost their permanent jobs through downsizing. Some now work as independent contractors, i.e. for themselves, trading independence for servitude. That means that they no longer have paid benefits, insurance, vacations. If they are not independent contractors, then they may be temporary employees. The temp workers often find themselves in jobs just up to the point where the company will have to keep them permanently or let them go, and then they lose their jobs and begin all over again. Frequently the temp jobs have been part-time work in fields that are a mark-down from the profession they formerly claimed as theirs. ObamaCare has exacerbated this situation with demands to provide health benefits for full-time workers. Companies avoid that requirement by cutting employees back to part-time status.

More and more mothers and fathers find themselves putting in twelve-hour workdays because they are working for salary; and if they don't meet the requirements of the company, the company will give the job to someone else. As temps, they work extra hours to please with the expectation they may be rewarded with a permanent job. When they are "laid off" instead, or their contract is terminated, they begin the pattern again, joining the multitude of job seekers. We don't really have an accurate figure for unemployment because so many people have joined the ranks of the permanently unemployed and just stopped looking.

No protection

We have euphemized our language to de-emphasize the pain: "down-sized," "laid-off," instead of fired and discarded. Unions came into being to protect workers against abuse. They were effective. Now there is a stigma attached to being a blue-collar worker, to being unionized. The governor of Wisconsin, with enormous conflict, finally won against the unions in that State. The Teacher Union negotiations with the City of Chicago were brutal, and in the end both sides lost.

Where do people go if they are not educated and trained to move with the technological advances of our American society? Not very far. Yet for the first time since the introduction of the GI Bill after World War II, there is a debate about the value of a College Degree. Law Schools are finding it hard to attract new students because so many law school graduates find themselves unemployed and burdened with huge debt. The debt for a four-year degree may put huge burdens on graduates for the next twenty years, and the income does not warrant the debt.

Downsized expectations

How many families today have the expectation that they will take a two-week paid vacation and go somewhere? How many families expect to spend long summer evenings in the back yard playing ball and talking with the neighbors. How many families would have time to use a front porch if they had one? Parents pick their children up from day care, stop at the supermarket or a fast food place, throw some food on the table, help the children with homework and put them to bed, and then fall asleep exhausted, knowing they'll have just a few hours of rest before they begin their early-morning roller coaster again: the hamster wheel. To add to burden, *The Wall Street Journal* reports in July of 2016 the child care expenses alone have climbed nearly twice as fast as overall prices since the recession ended in 2009, increasing the cost of raising a child born in 2013 until age 18 to a projected $245,340, nearly five years of income for the median U.S household. The jump in overall inflation-adjusted costs mainly reflects increases in child-care, education and health-care expenses.[6]

The rat race

As fewer and fewer homes have two parents to share the burden of raising and feeding a family, in addition to the burden of "just getting by," of "making ends meet," individuals carry the burden of guilt because they're not really doing anything as well as they would like or think they should. Women stick with the family because they feel the guiltiest. If the marriage didn't work out, there must be something they did wrong. People resent other people just because they "have a life." 85% of black women are single parents carrying the entire burden for their families. Please notice I have used the word "burden" three times in just one paragraph. This is what Bob Kiyosaki in his book, *Rich Dad, Poor Dad*,[7] typifies as the rat race. We are like rats in a maze, "making ends meet," and so bound up in it that we can't step back from the drama of the situation to get it under control, to give ourselves space for change. We are hamsters bound to the wheel.

Getting and spending

I will use myself as an example. My children are grown and gone. I know I can best serve myself by arising early each morning and setting aside the best part of my day for writing. This is when my mind is clear, when the phone doesn't ring, when I can be creative and expressive, without interruption. Yet for years I put myself in a position where I took jobs that required early morning hours, when I had to be places and do things early in the morning, making it impossible for me to use the best time for the best work. It became as Wordsworth observes in "The World Is Too Much With Us": "Getting and spending we lay waste our powers/ Little we see in Nature that is ours./ We have given our hearts away, a sordid boon!"

Nose to the grindstone

It was easy for me to justify the early morning hours, the job that made the income I needed to survive, but it was strangling my spirit and misdirecting my energy. The activity came out fear, fear there wouldn't be enough, fear that if I left a gap, nothing might come to fill it, fear that I had to grab on to this fill-in job to "make ends meet." That is a race consciousness *old saying*, "to make ends meet." It suggests that we might barely be able to put enough together, but there will never be more than enough. The perceived need to "make ends meet" becomes a self-fulfilling prophecy. When you barely "make ends meet," the activity becomes an end in itself. It does not stretch outward or inward. It goes nowhere. When ends are meeting, there is no horizon. In order to "make ends meet," one must "stick one's nose to the grindstone," another *old saying*. Examine that image. With the nose attached to the grindstone, there is no looking up, no looking out, only mindless repetitious activity: stuck on the hamster wheel.

Confused and afraid

Most Americans are working so hard because they have goals to achieve. Many have just given up. Yet, when we come at our own experience from scarcity thinking, with the thought that there isn't quite enough, then it is difficult for us to have faith that what we expect, what we wish, what we entertain in our heart of heart can really come true. This is called confusion. On the one hand we may set goals based on dreams; but on the other hand, we are saying the goals are unachievable and the dreams are pie in the sky. An object, for instance a car, cannot travel in two directions at the same time. We wouldn't even attempt it. Yet, how often do we live our life in such a way that the "push me-pull me" is constantly at war on our spirit. It reminds me of the farm boy who was drafted in the army. The sergeant was putting them through a drill, "Forward march," "Rear march," "Forward march," "Rear march." The boy went over and sat down. The sergeant asked, "Just what do you think you're doing?" The boy replied, "I ain't doin' nothin' until you make up your mind what you're doin."

From the garage door to the front porch

You can probably tell that I still have "energy" around this part of my sentence. As we explore Fuller's concepts, however, we will find that if we let go of false life--savers, "piano tops," use leverage and synergy effectively, know our big picture, and set our navigation path, we can begin to get off the hamster wheel. We can move into a position of control over our lives, over our destiny: *reset, reboot, replant.* It can take us from the garage door to the front porch. If "making ends meet" is a ruling force of your daily life, controls your actions, binds you to the hamster wheel, acknowledge it right here and right now. Also acknowledge you have the ability, one step at a time, to take control, to move into the center, to direct your daily traffic, to reign sovereign over your state.

"My children," said an old man to his boys scared by a figure in the dark entry, "my children, you will never see anything worse than yourselves." As in dreams, so in the scarcely less fluid events of the world every man sees himself in colossal, without knowing that it is himself. The good, compared to the evil which he sees, is as his own good to his own evil.

Emerson, "Spiritual Laws" [1]

Crime and punishment grow out of one stem. Punishment is a fruit that unsuspected ripens within the flower of the pleasure that concealed it. Cause and effect, means and ends, seed and fruit, cannot be severed; for the effect already blooms in the cause, the end preexists in the means, the fruit in the seed.

Emerson, "Compensation" [2]

INHERENT EVIL

Witness the black veil

NATHANIAL HAWTHORNE, ONE of the early articulators of the American Puritanism, may not have intended to make us scared of ourselves, but he certainly has that effect on me. In Hawthorne's story "The Minister's Black Veil," a young minister begins to wear a black crepe veil over his face. It becomes his emblem, his identity. He refuses to take it off for anyone, even his fiancée. The veil never changes, but the reaction of his observers has a curious evolution. At first the people in the village and in his congregation regard it with horror and revulsion. Then they become attracted to it, even obsessed with it. People come from far away to witness the black veil, and those on their deathbed wait to die for the minister with his veil to appear. Just before the minister's own death, another pastor suggests that he remove the veil, saying, "Before the veil of eternity be lifted, let me cast aside this black veil from your face!"

"Never!" cries out the minister, "On earth, never!"[3]

The condemnation

Hawthorne tells us the "black veil hung down, awful, at that last moment, in the gathered terrors of a lifetime. In his dying words, the minister speaks forth his condemnation upon all mankind:

> 'Tremble also at each other! Have men avoided me, and women shown no pity, and children screamed and fled, only for my black veil? What, but the mystery which it obscurely typifies, has made this piece of crepe so awful? When the friend shows his inmost heart to his friend; the lover to his best beloved; when man does not vainly shrink from the eye of his Creator, loathsomely treasuring upon the secret of his sin; then deem me a monster for the symbol beneath which I have lived and die. I look around me, and, lo! On every visage a Black Veil!'[4]

For one of my Introduction to Literature classes, I bought some black crepe fabric and cut it into veils. The students were divided into two groups and took turns wearing the veil and speaking with a partner. They found that when they wore the veil, they felt power, control, and intimidation over the other person. It felt as if their eyes could penetrate into the hearts of the unveiled. Those without the veil felt uneasy, anxious, as if there were a darkness in their secret life that perhaps they hadn't yet revealed even to themselves. It was eerie.

Young Goodman Brown
Lost Faith

In yet another story, Hawthorne takes "Young Goodman Brown" out into the forest. Young Goodman Brown is a fine, respected citizen, newly married to his lovely wife, Faith. He leaves Faith at home when he goes into the forest, for there he meets the Devil, his guide, dressed much as himself but carrying a staff that is a black serpent. Deep within the forest, he and the Devil meet the inhabitants. To his surprise, he finds the people of his village, those whom he regarded as the most upright of citizens, even Goody Cloyse who taught him catechism. There he even finds his wife, Faith, in her ribbons; and shocked to find her at such a cabal, he utters, "My Faith is gone!"

Hawthorne tells us at this awful moment, Young Goodman Brown looked into the horror of the human soul: "The whole forest was peopled with frightful sounds – the creaking of the trees, the howling of wild beasts, and the yell of Indians; while sometimes the wind tolled like a distant church bell, and sometimes gave a broad roar around the traveler, as if all Nature were laughing him to scorn. But he was himself the chief horror of the scene, and shrank not from its other horrors."[5]

None escape.

The Devil

'This night it shall be granted you to know their secret deeds: how hoary-hearted elders of the church have whispered wanton words to the young maids of their households; how many a woman, eager for widows' weeds, has given her husband a drink at bedtime and let him sleep his last sleep in her bosom; how beardless youths have made haste to inherit their father's wealth; and how fair damsels – blush not, sweet ones – have dug little graves in the garden, and bidden me, the sole guest, to an infant's funeral. By the sympathy of your human hearts for sin ye shall scent out all the places whether in church, bed-chamber, street, field, or forest – where crime has been committed, and shall exult to behold the whole earth one stain of guilt, one mighty blood spot. Far more than this. It shall be yours to penetrate, in every bosom, the deep mystery of sin, the fountain of all wicked arts, and which inexhaustibly supplies more evil impulses than human power - than my power at its utmost - can make manifest in deeds."[6]

Hawthorne asks, "Had Goodman Brown fallen asleep in the forest and only dreamed a wild dream of a witch-meeting?" If it were so, it was "a dream of evil omen for young Goodman Brown. A stern, a sad, a darkly meditative, a distrustful, if not a desperate man did he become from the night of that fearful dream." And if it were a dream, is it any less real than waking up and finding yourself a cockroach?

Nothing changed

Deep in the American psyche is this race consciousness of inherent evil, which Hawthorne articulates, symbolized by the black veil, by the dark forest where we hide our sinful selves. Hawthorne published "Young Goodman Brown" in 1835 and "The Minister's Black Veil" in 1837. Note how the "sins" described in the witch meeting not only prevail but are media blitzes today: imposition of sexual advances by men in power positions on vulnerable young women; induction of early death by family members or care givers; murder to inherit wealth; abortion.

A Four-Star General resigned as Head of the CIA for sharing classified information with his sexual liaison. A President was impeached for failing to admit sexual dalliance with a young woman in the oval office. A woman called "the gypsy" was arrested after the sudden death of the fifth husband to die under similar circumstances, each husband wealthy and 40- 50 years older. A high school counselor was indicted for giving abortion information to a student. The late Dr. Kavorkian testified on his own behalf in his trial for performing self-assisted suicides. The circumstances are the same. We speak of these situations today as problems to be dealt with by law or prison or by redefinition of ethical standards. Yet, Hawthorne would tell us we are all in prison already, for on every visage is the black veil.

Collective guilt

In the race consciousness of guilt held collectively in our unconscious, these are the sins of the father visited on the son, our inheritance. We can shrug them off intellectually, but psychologically, emotionally, they have a grip. Even though I spent years indoctrinating myself in a religious faith that teaches there is no hell to save us from and no heaven to send us to, that there is no evil, only a deviation from perfection, I always have this lingering suspicion that God set us up, made us this way, even treats us as a cruel joke.

Assault of horror and tragedy

Recently it has seemed as if the race consciousness and the "climate of opinion" have joined together in an articulation of horror. We hear it on the radio, watch it in the news, in a mass murder of attorneys in San Francisco and of brokers in Atlanta, Georgia; in the Columbine High School massacre in Littleton, Colorado; in the massacre at a Denver theater; in the elementary school massacre in Connecticut; in shootings at a Jewish day-care center in Los Angeles, in a bar in Orlando, on the street of Dallas. Although statistically violent crime performed by juveniles is declining, our climate of opinion, however, is determined by what the media chooses to show us. The media is relentless in its coverage of mass tragedies and celebrates anniversaries with replays. In the novel *The Luckiest Girl Alive*, Jessica Knoll reports a gang rape and a Columbine-inspired massacre. It has hit the top of the *New York Times* Bestseller List and will soon be made into a movie. This follows on the heels of Gillian Flynn's *Gone Girl*, another *New York Times* Bestseller made into a creepy movie. Hawthorne's "fearful dream" sucks us into its abyss.

In search of good news

There is an alternative light at the end of the tunnel, the new moon that follows the dark of the moon. We can balance the Columbine High School tragedy with the publication of *The Freedom Writers Diary*, an anthology of accounts written by Wilson High School students in Long Beach, California. These students were all potential dropouts, unsupported at home and living on the fringe. They were turned around by a teacher, Erin Gruwell, who was played by Hilary Swank in the movie *Freedom Writers*. In *The Freedom Writers Diary* these students, all high school graduates, tell about how they overcame the abuses of their childhood and found hope from hardship, from a father who sold the family home to buy crack to a grandfather who molested his granddaughter.

These students received $250,000 from John Tu of Kingston Technology in Fountain Valley, California, the entrepreneur who has twice distinguished himself by sharing enormous bonuses with his employees. He supported the Tolerance Tour to Europe for this group of young men and women. A documentary movie follows the entire group on another trip to Washington, D.C. Erin Gruwell now has the Freedom Writer's Foundation and teaches other teachers to do what she did. The first Ph.D. from that Wilson High School class has earned her degree. This good news doesn't "sell" as well as the preoccupation with psychopathic behavior, but at least it is part of our public discourse and receiving attention.

Laying blame

When something horrible occurs, we search for someone to blame. Columbine's atrocities were blamed on the videos the killers watched. Yet millions of people have watched the same videos and have not murdered anyone. Today we deal with Isis, with individuals self-radicalized over the internet acting as "lone wolves" to destroy the infidels in San Bernardino, in Orlando, at Bastille Day Fireworks in Nice. We deal with protests and sniper attacks in retaliation for police shootings. There lurks in our consciousness both the assumption and the fear that we all have inherited a disposition for evil that might be awakened if we let down our guard.

Our climate of opinion on the one hand, invokes the sanctity of childhood, the purity of children, the redemptive ability of the unspoiled human spirit that may momentarily be misdirected. On the other hand, our climate of opinion celebrates deviance and depravity. When I was growing up, people used to say that the worst thing that could happen to a juvenile delinquent was to get caught. In fact, here again the language expresses the climate of opinion. An adult killer is a criminal; a killer who is a child is a juvenile delinquent, one who left the path. It was thought that exposure of the juvenile to the criminal justice system with "hard criminals" would corrupt the juvenile even further.

In our Columbine and Wilson High School examples, we are confronted with two groups of children, one group from respectable families who express the most incredible evil; and another group who have been subjected to unspeakable abuse, yet who not only overcome it, but also triumph over it. Underlying both instances, however, is the recognition that the propensity for evil exists in the human spirit, waiting to be let out, a bad seed.

From acorn to tree

We know the tiny acorn within the shell contains within it the essence of beingness of the tree, is the truth of the tree within the seed. In the course of growing down, putting out roots, then growing up, putting forth branches, the tree is subjected to the vicissitudes of nature, to variations of light and dark, water and drought, cold and warmth. The truth of the being of that tree is pre-determined, but the climate changes. The tree in becoming who it is must learn to deal with the climate, must adapt. It never deviates from its self-knowledge, but all of its self-knowledge may not be expressed if the demands of the environment do not require it.

Self-knowingness

Our human path here is much the same. Our spirit knows itself, knows the truth of itself. Yet it is born into a climate of opinion that is forever changing and adapting, forever sending forth messages which may be true or may be false, but they have an effect on us. It is that spark within us at birth, so often extinguished by circumstance, waiting to be discovered if we push that "reset "button, if we have the fortitude to "reboot." The message from our Puritan ancestry into which we were born, however, tells us that man's inherent proclivity for evil makes suffering inevitable, that our goodness will only be as good as our ability to overcome temptation, that our life here on earth is meant to be a trial, that only the afterlife is of importance, and that the life we live here is lived for the hereafter rather than for the present. In fact, to be concerned with the present is self-indulgent.

Our choice

If we accept this thinking, we may find it hard to get out of bed in the morning. What's the point? As we will find when we begin to explore the new moon ideological framework, we cannot "change one iota of yesterday," but we can come out of the darkness into the light. I accept that I carry around Hawthorne, the race consciousness, the climate of opinion created by the media. Having accepted that awareness, I can also now release it, because it does not serve me. I am at choice to *reset*, r*eboot* and *replant*. I can choose to nurture my mind and spirit with positive thoughts, with inspirational words, with acts of courage and kindness, with people who demonstrate purpose and direction. It may be a simple thing like playing a tape in the car rather than listening to the news or talk radio, reading with a child, stopping by to visit a friend, participating in a community project, or even taking my dog for a walk. I hope you choose to do the same.

Nothing seems so easy as to speak and to be understood. Yet a man may come to find that the strongest of defenses and of ties – that he has been understood; and he who has received an opinion may come to find it the most inconvenient of bonds.

Emerson, "Spiritual Laws"[1]

Ah, but a man's reach should exceed his grasp,
Or what's a heaven for?

Robert Browning, "Andrea del Sarto" ll. 97-98

For thence, --a paradox
Which comforts while it mocks,
Shall life succeed in that it seems to fail:
What I aspired to be,
And was not, comforts me:
A brute I might have been, but would not sink
I' the scale.

Robert Browning, "Rabbi Ben Ezra," ll. 38-43

LIMITS: LIVING SOMEONE ELSE'S IDEA

First adolescent love

IN *DUBLINERS* JAMES Joyce tells a poignant story of adolescent puppy love, "Araby." The speaker in the story has just discovered that he prefers watching out the window for his friend, Mangan's, older sister than playing with his friends in the blind alley where their homes are located: "Her name sprang to my lips at moments in strange prayers and praises which I myself did not understand. My eyes were often full of tears (I could not tell why) and at times a flood from my heart seemed to pour itself out into my bosom. I thought little of the future. I did not know whether I would ever speak to her or not or, if I spoke to her, how I could tell her of my confused adoration. But my body was like a harp and her words and gestures were like fingers running upon the wires."[2]

The young damsel, aware of the attention, plays with the boy when she encounters him from her front porch. "She asked me was I going to Araby. I forgot whether I answered yes or no. It would be a splendid bazaar, she said she would love to go." As she speaks, she twists her silver bracelet "round and round her wrist. She could not go, she said, because there would be a retreat that week in her convent." He promises that if he goes, he will bring her something.

Temptation to quest

It becomes the boy's obsession to go to Araby to buy her a gift. The very name of "Araby" evokes all that is exotic and romantic. On the designated day, his uncle's payday, he waits in pain for the money for his train ride to Araby. It gets later and later; and when his uncle finally comes home, a true Dubliner, he has been drinking and makes coarse jokes. The boy rushes out of the house, gets on the train, and arrives at Araby only to find it closing down: "I recognized a silence like that which pervades a church after a service." The boy frantically looks for a gift, finding he hasn't enough money to buy anything. He stops at a stall and interrupts a young man and woman engaged in love talk. She asks him if he wishes to buy something. "The tone of her voice was not encouraging." He looks at the "great jars that stood like eastern guards at either side of the dark entrance to the stall and murmured, 'No, thank you.'" As he walks away, he "allowed the two pennies to fall against the sixpence in my pocket." As he leaves, Joyce tells us, "Gazing up into the darkness I saw myself as a creature driven and derided by vanity; and my eyes burned with anguish and anger."

The humiliation of failure

This is the mature James Joyce observing his adolescent self, recalling the bitter memory of this impotent moment. Mangan's sister is long gone in real life, probably married with twelve children, but she is seared into Joyce's memory. How many of us have attempted to bring a gift from Araby to someone who long ago forgot she ever mentioned wanting it?

How many of us have returned over and over to Araby, seeking the extraordinary, humiliated by our failure, acting out a pattern of behavior for which the initial cause long ago evaporated? In the subtle exchange of communication, whether sensualized and eroticized, as for Joyce, or whether accepted by one in a subordinate position from one in control, the desire to please and satisfy someone else may impose limits for a lifetime. We may keep acting out someone else's dream and never come up with our own. This is a familiar pattern in adolescence, and many of us never graduate and grow up.

Must and should

In my work with people, I have discovered that the more developed the ego function, the more obligations and responsibilities take the forefront, the more "must" and "should" enter their vocabularies. We make a distinction, however, between the self-defining and self-empowering fulfillment of obligations and responsibilities and the fulfillment of the obligations and responsibilities repeated again and again with no *apparent* inner logic: the hamster wheel. In the latter instance, one may be acting out of some felt need to respond to some distant message, long ago forgotten by the messenger. It may, in fact, have been a passing, incidental expression of the messenger that was then taken to heart by the recipient, blown out of proportion, and elevated to serve as a *raison d'etre*. Mangan's sister forgot about Araby long ago. James Joyce, as a mature adult is still going there. As Emerson says "He who has received an opinion may come to find it the most inconvenient of bonds."

Rage for order

The physicist Heisenberg noted that in the process of any interaction, in scientific observation, the observer is linked to the object being observed, and the object is altered by the process of the observation. To carry this insight into our everyday activities and affairs, we must say that in the process of even the briefest of conversations, the listener and the speaker are altered by the connection. Do we have any desire in life greater than to understand and to be understood?

There is a drive for order, for the system to be working efficiently, for the organism to be in harmony and peace. As human beings, we are highly complex organisms. When one part of the organism is in disharmony, is not functioning efficiently, the whole organism rushes to that place to repair, to take care, to re-establish the *status quo*. Physically, our bodies are programmed to do this. When we cut ourselves, the organism repairs the wound, fills it back up, covers it over. We do not have to say to our bodies, this is what we want to happen. Our bodies know.

The unarticulated message

Our minds react similarly. When we are confused, we are ill at ease, nervous. We use words such as "wander" to describe the state of confusion; because when we are confused, we lack direction. We lose a sense of who we are, and we do not know where we are going. As we learn, we experience temporary confusion, a time when our minds are groping to put together a myriad of impulses and ideas and to re-organize them into a state we can comprehend. We grow as we grope for comprehension, seeking the re-organization of data into an understandable context.

In the same way, we seek to be understood, we seek to communicate our entire beings. If words are only seven percent of communication, the auditory sound of our voices fifty-five percent, and our body language thirty-eight percent, then in a conversation the exchange taking place is an actual exchange of essence, of aura, of energy fields. When Mangan's sister twirls her bracelet, she sexualizes her desire to go to Araby, and the boy is aroused subconsciously, not consciously aware. She knows what she is doing; she plays with him. We know when we have been understood, when we have been heard, when we have been felt, when we have been seen. A child quickly learns to understand the message of the parent, articulated or not.

The child knows not only what acceptable behavior is, but also how the child stands in relation to the parent.

The parents' messages

For much of my life, I was acting out my parents' messages. Just as the son in "The Judgment" saw his sickly father as a "giant of a man," so did I perceive my parents. My mother was a very pretty woman. She always spent what seemed like hours each day primping and making herself more pretty. One of my earliest memories is of a Luzier representative, an early Mary Kay, coming to our house and selling my mother cosmetics over the kitchen table. As I write this the smell of my mother from my childhood comes back to me. No one was supposed to be more pretty than mother. That included me. My father was a very smart man. He prided himself on his ability to think, to know, and to solve problems. He had a photographic memory and could synthesize information effectively. No one was supposed to be smarter than my father. One could be smart, for that would be a reflection of him in me, but one could not be smarter.

Knowing the limits

So mother would dress me up like her little doll. She made me sit still every night so that she could set my hair in long curls. Often she would dress me in an outfit like hers, having matching outfits custom-made for us. She always looked better in them than I did. Those were the rules. In my mind, it was acceptable to look good, but not better. It was acceptable to be bright, but not brighter. One could be oneself up to a point, but one could not exceed that point, for it was reserved for the parent. Those were my limits.

When I attended elementary school, I was a very smart little girl. The teachers and students all acknowledged that. Also, I was a leader. Although I was chubby, I was elected as a cheerleader and even had a boyfriend. Because I had enough to eat, enough to wear, and a sense of achievement, I thought that I was ok. It did not seem strange and unusual to me that each week I had three clean dresses. I would wear one on Monday, another on Tuesday, and the third on Wednesday. Then I could choose two of the three to wear a second time on Thursday and Friday.

Since this was the way we did things at our house, and since I was always clean, this is how I thought life was supposed to be. Mother would come to visit on parent-visitation day, and the children would say to me, "Your mother is so pretty. It's too bad you don't look like her." And I would know that both at school and at home, mother was prettier. My principal had been my father's teacher in elementary school, and she considered my father the most brilliant student she ever had. So I knew my limit: I could be smart, but not so smart as my father.

Acting the limits out

When I left elementary school, I went to a junior high that brought together students from four elementary schools: Lincoln, Jefferson, McKinley, and Garfield. You can see my community was strong on presidential leadership. There I discovered McKinley and Jefferson, the two elementary schools I had attended, were both on the "wrong side of the tracks." Where I had been "good enough" but not better than my parents at McKinley, now I wasn't even "good enough." My boyfriend already had a girlfriend from Garfield, and I was just an overweight, badly dressed, smart but outcast girl from McKinley. Because our sixth grade teacher, Mrs. Kauffman, had taught us to stand and recite, I continued to do that in my classes. Finally, Miss Bierlein, in my seventh grade math class, told me it wasn't necessary to stand. I felt completely humiliated.

There was nowhere to go but inside. My outer self was disconnected from my inner self. I didn't understand, and I certainly was not understood. The only place I could find harmony and peace was in the imagination, in books, and I spent all of my time reading. My mother resented my reading. She constantly said to me, "Get your nose out of that book." Yet when the study hall teacher came to look at an apartment we had for rent, and when she told my mother I had the highest achievement scores in the seventh grade, then mother determined I must be first and stay first. I was caught in a constant state of confusion because I was supposed to get my nose out of the book, yet I was supposed to be first, which meant that I had to have my nose in a book. But my father was first, so how could I be first?

Unintentional messengers

I am sharing this with you because, in retrospect, I realize my parents were just being themselves. The messages I integrated into my emotional and intellectual life were the ones I interpreted, absorbed, and acted upon. I did it. They didn't. Yet I am like James Joyce, in maturity observing my adolescent self. It takes us back to the sentencing. The limits we place on ourselves are of our own making, our own acceptance of messages often delivered quite without deliberation and intent by the deliverer who was just being himself.

Self sabotage

I won't burden you with an inventory of the times in my life that I have acted upon my perceived limits, some seemingly incongruent self-sabotage to keep me from being first or best. I was married at the age of 22. I had completed both a B.A. and M.A. from the University of Michigan, putting myself through school with scholarships and part-time jobs. My new husband proceeded right after the wedding to make me get rid of my clothes. The words "make me" today give me a shudder, but then they were a part of my vocabulary. I had dressed a little exotically. Those were the "beatnik" days, and I carried a green book bag and wore black tights. Most of my clothes were purchased by my mother "on sale," and she had an eye for the unusual. I remember in particular two extraordinary, quilted full skirts. One was purple with large, brilliantly colored flowers and the other was black with large gold coin-shaped dots. I loved wearing those skirts, and I recall I had a fitted black coat to wear over them.

When my husband started getting rid of my clothes, it didn't even occur to me that how I dressed must have, in part, attracted him to me. I didn't express a single word of indignation. In retrospect, looking back at this still adolescent self from a standpoint of maturity, I realize his message to me was clearly that I wasn't good enough. I sought out someone who would give me that message so I could stay within my self-imposed limit, so I could fulfill *my sentence*.

Sentences generalized

This ability to self-sabotage as we fulfill *our sentence* may manifest in the financial realm as well. Frequently a pattern will emerge for an individual who achieves a level of income almost as high as his parents'. When the income is about to exceed the parents' level, he does something to get himself demoted or fired, some self-defeating act, a self-sabotage, because unconsciously he fears being better than, or outdoing, his parents. The message that individual took in from his parents is he is not to be better. It may be the parents never consciously meant to send that message, but they were acting out, living out their own response to *their sentence* in life.

For many of us living out a life sentence, living out someone else's dream, or living out someone else's limits, may be strangling our ability to move forward in our own lives. We will be exploring "piano tops" as we *reset.* When we cling to "piano tops," we are hanging on to a lifesaver that has ceased to serve us effectively.

You may ask yourself at this point whether the dream you have for the unfolding of your life originates in you, or whether you got it from someone else. When you talk to yourself, is it your voice or someone else's? How did you come to formulate and to own your vision for your life? If it isn't yours, what must you change for you to make it your own?

For, what with my whole world-wide wandering,
What with my search drawn out thro' years, my hope
Dwindled into a ghost not fit to cope
With that obstreperous joy success would bring,
I hardly tried now to rebuke the spring
My heart made, finding failure in its scope.

Robert Browning, "Childe Roland to the Dark Tower Came" ll. 19-24

Tho' much is taken, much abides; and tho'
We are not now that strength which in old days
Moved earth and heaven, that which we are, we are,--
One equal temper of heroic hearts,
Made weak by time and fate, but strong in will
To strive, to seek, to find, and not to yield.

Tennyson, "Ulysses," ll. 66-71

TOO EASY: THE OXEN AND THE EAGLE

Each man has his own vocation. The talent is the call. There is one direction in which all space is open to him. He has faculties silently inviting him thither to endless exertion. He is like a ship in a river; he runs against obstructions on every side but one, on that side all obstruction is taken away and he sweeps serenely over a deepening channel into an infinite sea.

Emerson, "Spiritual Laws"[1]

Your boat

Successfully navigated?

Isn't that a great picture Emerson paints for us? Here you are, cast in this mighty metaphor with a great emotional rush of freedom, confidence and self assurance, at the triumphant end of the movie, *This Is Your Life*, in full Technicolor, riding your little boat into the sunset, fully able to enter any port at any time and to have exactly what you need.

Wow! Or does the voice inside you say, "Oops, there's something wrong with this picture?" We talk of walking the road of life; we are pathfinders. It is one thing to be walking or finding, but it's quite another to just be sweeping through deep water into an infinite whatever. This infinite is unknown.

Out of control?

Does the voice inside of you say, "Wait a minute. How do I know I can stop when I need to? How do I know the boat won't get away from me? How do I know this isn't a trick, a mistake? How do I know I won't get off course? Haven't I heard all my life that if it's easy, it isn't worth doing?" Poets write poems about the importance of what's difficult.

Fit to fail?

In "Childe Roland to the Dark Tower came," Robert Browning tells us we must be fit to fail. That is how we must measure ourselves. We truly win when we open ourselves to the full possibility of failure. That is essential to run for any office, to compete in any event. There will be only one winner. Tennyson concludes "Ulysses" with the line most quoted in "Commencement" addresses, the quest of life: "To strive, to seek, to find, and not to yield." The underlying assumption is we never quite reach the far goal. We know who we are from the big stretch, the achievement not quite realized. Browning sums it up when he admonishes us:

> Far better to aim for 1000 and miss it by one,
> Than to aim for 500 and make it.

Too easy

Emerson meant to instruct and to inspire us with this analogy of the boat sailing so easily; for he says when we are doing the right work, following the right vocation, the path opens effortlessly before us. How easy is it to accept this inspiration. Your grandmother may have told you, "Little boats belong close to shore." This implies, "If you go out to sea, how will you get back?" The current runs toward the sea. Your little boat won't be able to navigate against the current to get back where you were. It's a total risk. Once you've moved with the flow, there's no returning to safety, to where you were.

Besides

Besides, if it's easy, it must not be important. Why "besides?" Shakespeare put many of his most important statements in "asides." Did you ever notice how, when you speak of the thing most important to you, you may interject a "Well, besides?" Have you ever said such things as, "The weather's really too lousy for us to go; besides, I don't have anything to wear anyhow." Or have you ever said, "I don't know why I overslept and missed the interview; besides, they wouldn't have hired me anyway." When we say "besides," we are really expressing the most important thing to us. "Besides, I don't have anything to wear" really means, "I don't feel good about the way I look in any of my clothes." "Besides, they wouldn't have hired me anyway," really says, "I don't feel I have the qualifications I need to do the work I'd like to do." Often a "besides" is a little cry from inside us that says either "I'm not enough," or "I might not be enough."

Staying stuck

"Besides" indicates the fear of letting go, the fear of moving beyond the obstacle, because the obstacle, the staying stuck is familiar. We feel grounded in the marsh or the swamp, knowing we might sink, but at least we won't be swept away. It takes tremendous courage to do what's easy, apparent, and comfortable; because when we do that, we take full responsibility for our little ship, our little self.

Adam and Eve: the first stuck

Being human is being stuck. That is one of those things I learned on the front porch. It may have been as early as the summer before the fourth grade when I went on the bus every morning to the Tabernacle Bible School. God set us up to be stuck. That is what original sin is all about. I eat apples, but I didn't eat *the apple*. Eve ate *the apple*, and ever since, we have all been stuck. Although I know that the writing of the first two books of Genesis was at least three centuries apart, when I go back to the first two chapters of Genesis, as a reader, not as a

Biblical scholar, I feel set up. This is how I interpret the human condition described in the first two chapters of *Genesis*.

God-given dominion

When God has finished his work, when he has created man and woman in his own image, he speaks, "Let us make man in our image, after our likeness: and let them have dominion over the fish of the sea, and over the fowl of the air, and over the cattle, and over all the earth, and over every creeping thing that creepeth upon the earth." And then God blessed them and he said to them, "Be fruitful, and multiply, and replenish the earth, and subdue: and have dominion over the fish of the sea, and over the fowl of the air, and over every living thing that moveth upon the earth." This is the first chapter of *Genesis*. God repeats our dominion twice.

Not really

Then we come to the second chapter. God just gave us "dominion," and now he already takes it away. God, not man, determined to create hardship; for in the second chapter of *Genesis*, before God has made man, he does the planting of his Garden of Eden: "And the Lord God planted a garden eastward in Eden; and there he put the man whom he had formed. And out of the ground made the Lord God to grow every tree that is pleasant to the sight, and good for food; the tree of life also in the midst of the garden, and the tree of knowledge of good and evil."

God no longer direct

Suddenly God no longer "goes direct." He who spoke directly about creeping and flying and dominion now has Adam speak of the birth of Eve. It is Adam who states, "This is now bone of my bones and flesh of my flesh: she shall be called Woman, because she was taken out of man." God evades the issue that determines the entire future of man in his intercourse with other men. He puts it in the mouths of the serpent and the first woman, both acknowledged as God's creations. Indeed, we are told by some strange, unidentified, now omniscient speaker, "The serpent was more subtle than any beast of the field which the Lord God had made."

Eve and the serpent

Only when the serpent and Eve talk, do we learn of the consequences of eating of the tree in the middle of the garden, the "tree of knowledge of good and evil." However could it be that this serpent and this woman, newly made and introduced to life, could even conceive of death, of the knowing of good and evil? All of this is the creation of God. He planted the garden. God knows whom and what he has created, and he fully anticipates the results. He is waiting in the wings to condemn his creation for doing what he knew all along it would do.

Master and slave

This dilemma has plagued and delighted philosophers and theologians for centuries. Perhaps Hegel saw it most clearly when he determined that God from the beginning wanted a master and slave situation, wanted to be amused by the antics of man and pleased by his position of authority over man. The arguments for free will are a cruel joke we play on ourselves to explain the human condition, our rationalization of the trap laid for us.

Man's theistic rendering

The story in *Genesis* comes out of an oral tradition, not as the actual spoken word of God, but rather as the manifestation of man's attempt to define himself and to explain how he got the way he is. Man in the Bible creates God in the image and the likeness of himself. This is man's rendition of the way he thinks God spoke. He is a powerful father, somewhere up above, looking down and keeping score. Both stories in *Genesis* express an explanation arising from our race consciousness, evolved as man has evolved, a statement of why we must struggle in a universe that is so perfect in every way, and why man, more than any other creature, must be aware of this struggle, must be pulled apart by it in his mind and soul. We thrust the responsibility on a higher power; because if we must accept that responsibility for ourselves, we are crushed by our weakness, by our susceptibility to get ourselves into trouble.

Life is supposed to be difficult. How can it be *not difficult*?

How then can we be comfortable as a little ship flowing out into the ocean? Everything in our collective unconscious, everything in our primordial memory cries out against this ease. Life is difficult. I remember in my adolescence playing Debussy's *Arpeggios* when I took piano lessons. The nun, Sister Mary Paula, my teacher, had starched white cuffs against her small wrists. When I hear Mozart or Haydn, the image of those cuffs represents to me cleanliness, precision, clarity. Sister Mary Paula told me to play the triplets against the eighth notes in the Debussy by saying, "Not difficult, not difficult, not difficult, not difficult." I can still hear the music of that phrase. Truthfully, the execution of this piece of music was difficult, but my mind took control of the situation, got my hands through it. Sometimes when I'm in the midst of a task that challenges me, I recite this musical phrase as an affirmation, as a touchstone: *not difficult.*

Fire and Ice.

Life is difficult. Survival is difficult. Hasn't the earth been ravaged by storms, by flood, by hail, by sleet, by fire, by ice. Man envisions the end of the planet as cataclysmic because the origin of the planet was cataclysmic. The planet emerged from a burst of energy, at once both creative and destructive. We carry this memory in our collective unconscious, at once knowing our origin and fearfully anticipating our end. "In the end is the beginning," says T. S. Eliot.

The poet Robert Frost says of "Fire and Ice":

> Some say the world will end in fire,
> Some say in ice.
> From what I've tasted of desire
> I hold with those who favor fire.

But if it had to perish twice,
I think I know enough of hate
To say that for destruction ice
Is also great
And would suffice.[2]

The cataclysmic memory

Thus, no matter what language we speak, whether we read or write, whether we are poets or philosophers, slaves or kings, tradesmen or warriors, seamen or tillers of the field, there is within us the cataclysmic memory. This is the pain relived in childbirth. We may or may not choose to believe the pain and fear came from eating the fruit of a forbidden tree. That depends upon one's theology. This memory, apart from any intellectual explanation, we share from an inner knowing, a consciousness so powerful that it is what truly distinguishes the human condition; for man alone among all creatures is able to articulate it and to share it in symbols and metaphors, in oxymorons, in paradoxes. In man alone the physical and the metaphysical become one.

Struggle familiar

And thus we cling to the familiar, to the known, because within us is the fear of the unknown. We cling to what is difficult, for in the struggle against it, we can feel defined; it gives us a grasp upon reality. We inherited the Judaic-Christian belief in struggle. As Americans, we got the Puritanical work ethic as well; and we are suspicious of anyone for whom life comes too easily.

Suffering punishment

We delight in hearing the horrors of the personal lives of people who express a natural talent. We expect our artists, writers, actors, and musicians to be "poor starving," because they can't expect to be paid if they love their work. I even recall a televised speech made by President George H. W. Bush at a conference on education when he articulated the assumption teachers shouldn't expect to make much money because they like what they do. We watch *Entertainment Tonight,* and we read the scandal-sheet headlines as we go through the supermarket. It reassures us the life of the rich and famous is wracked with pain and torment: crooked face lifts, alcohol and drug rehab, gigantic weight gains, family rejection, spousal abuse, bitter divorce. We watch various "judges" to see people in court more screwed up than we are. It justifies our chains, our submission to the yoke.

The oxen and the eagle

Man compares himself to the oxen in his metaphors, as often as he compares himself to the bird. As Hamlet says in his soliloquy, his "aside," when he tells the truth of himself, "My mind flies up. My thoughts remain below." Man is the oxen and the eagle, planted in the earth, inheritor of its struggle, with a mind that can carry him above and beyond, back to the true origins of his oneness with the creative impulse. How then can we be comfortable with the image of ourselves as a little ship flowing freely out to sea, unobstructed by difficulty?

Rediscovery: out at sea

What if paradoxically, for man is a paradox, we were to acknowledge the other memory that took us millions of years, perhaps billions to *rediscover*? We have all along been riding on a ship hurtling through space, unobstructed. *Re dis cover* is a wonderful word. We *re*, do again, *dis*, undo, what somehow we had *cover* ed, that is, put under wraps, never removing, never destroying, only getting out of sight, that is, out of the light of knowing, what has been true all along. We begin our voyage now as we began, "our end is our beginning." Can it be the struggles, the obstacles, originate in our minds? Changing one's mind is only a thought away.

When I heard the learn'd astronomer,
When the proofs, the figures, were ranged in columns before me,
When I was shown the charts and diagrams, to add, divide, and measure
them,
When I sitting heard the astronomer where he lectured with much
applause in the lecture room,
How soon unaccountable I became tired and sick,
Till rising and gliding out I wander'd off by myself,
In the mystical moist night-air and from time to time,
Look'd up in perfect silence at the stars.

Walt Whitman, 1865

This world is not Conclusion.
A species stands beyond—
Invisible, as Music—
But positive, as Sound—
It beckons, and it baffles—
Philosophy—don't know—
And through a Riddle, at the last—
Sagacity, must go—
To guess it, puzzles scholars—
To gain it, Men have borne
Contempt of Generations
And Crucifixion, shown—
Faith slips—and laughs, and rallies--
Blushes, if any see—
Plucks at a twig of Evidence—
And asks a Vane, the way—
Much Gesture, from the Pulpit—
Strong Hallelujahs roll—
Narcotics cannot still the Tooth
That nibbles at the soul—

Emily Dickinson, 1862

PART 2: A CONCEPTUAL FRAMEWORK

* We are all astronauts on a planet we understand by trial and error.

* We come at our knowledge in two ways

* Physical: Observation of physical and mathematical laws;

* Metaphysical: Mental application of observed and intuited perfection.

* We are links in the "Great Chain of Being," suspended watchers, seeking knowledge of perfection through intuited truth and rational analysis.

Having, then, made all these preparations, he did not wish to lose any time in putting his plan into effect, for he could not but blame himself for what the world was losing by his delay, so many were the wrongs that were to be righted, the grievances to be redressed, the abuses to be done away with, and the duties to be performed. Accordingly, without informing anyone of his intention and without letting anyone see him, he set out one morning before daybreak on one of those very hot days in July. Donning all his armor, mounting Rocinante, adjusting his ill-contrived helmet, bracing his shield on his arm, and taking up his lance, he sallied forth by the back gate of his stable yard into the open countryside. It was with great contentment and joy that he saw how easily he had made a beginning toward the fulfillment of his desire.

Cervantes, *Don Quixote*[1]

WE ARE ALL
ASTRONAUTS

Already an astronaut

IF THE IDEA of riding in Emerson's boat easily out to sea created anxiety, then just relax. You're already on board a ship easily and effortlessly traveling without obstruction. When R. Buckminster Fuller wrote his little book, *Operating Manual for Spaceship Earth*, he spoke of the planet we had not yet seen from the moon, awakening us so vividly to the visual and experiential awareness that we are all astronauts. Space travel is perfectly natural to us; we just didn't know it. We have all been taking for granted our sophisticated travel aboard this extraordinary vessel:

> Our little spaceship Earth is only eight thousand miles in diameter, which is almost a negligible dimension in the great vastness of space. Our nearest star – our energy-supplying mother-ship, the Sun – is ninety-two million miles away, and the nearest star is one hundred thousand

times further away. . . . Each minute we both spin at one hundred miles and zip in orbit at one thousand miles. This is a whole lot of spin and zip. When we launch our rocket space capsules at fifteen thousand miles an hour, that additional acceleration speed we give the rocket to attain its own orbit around our speeding Spaceship Earth is only one-fourth greater than the speed of our big planetary spaceship.

Spaceship Earth was so extraordinarily well invented and designed that to our knowledge humans have been on board it for two million years not even knowing that they were on board a ship. And our spaceship is so superbly designed as to be able to keep life regenerating on board despite the phenomenon, entropy, by which all local physical systems lose energy. So we have to obtain our biological life-regenerating energy from another spaceship – the sun.[2]

Space exploration natural evolution

This casts a new light on our perception of our selves. We are participants in a great adventure, and we didn't even know it. Adventure is our natural state. No wonder we love it so much. One would expect us to create rockets to carry us to other planets, while hurtling through space on our own ship. Space exploration is part of our natural evolution, of our own self-discovery. Just as man emerged from the water, a great amphibian, as Loren Eiseley describes in *The Immense Journey*, struggling up on shore to take his first breath of air, the first intake of life to suit man to earth, so also is it equally as natural for man to move outward into space, where he has always been. We are the only creatures who don the appropriate gear to go down to the depth of the sea and then out into space to push back the frontier. We thought it, imagined it, long before we could do it. We make waves, and we make roads, not where they've always been, but rather where we want them to be.

The road of life

We in America have always been fascinated with the image of man on the road of life, at the edge of the frontier. It may be, in part, because, unless we're indigenous Americans, we all came from immigrant roots. Somewhere in our past is at least one individual who was an inveterate risk taker, willing to leave everything familiar, comfortable, and valued behind. That individual was willing to test himself against all odds. It took resilience, courage, fortitude, persistence, intelligence, and faith. Our American western features this kind of hero. John Ford, one of our greatest directors of western films, likes to put his hero, alone on the road of life, against the backdrop of Monument Valley, with vast mountains and canyons in the background, encountering trials to his survival instinct and tests to his moral virtue. Events force him to act decisively.

The wary, wily, savvy searcher and winner

The man on the frontier masters his challenges because he is wary, wily, and savvy. The environment and its inhabitants are his to conquer. The western celebrates visionaries who look at a wood and see a lumberyard, who look at a trail and see a railroad, who look at a river and see a dam. The challenge and the quest beckon this man forward, whether in a covered wagon seeking a homestead or on a mule with a grubstake searching for gold. Two of John Ford's westerns are appropriately entitled: *The Searchers* and *How the West Was Won*. Searching and winning are the American way and embody the American Dream.

Space: the next frontier

When the frontier, defined and depicted by the Western, was too earth-bound, too limited, George Lucas and Stephen Spielberg moved it outward into space. Spielberg humanized it with *ET*, and Lucas "westernized" it with the *Star Wars* series. The backdrop has changed to outer space, but the issues are the same: good over evil, courage over fear, intelligence over error, mastery over tools. When George Lucas re-released *The Star Wars Trilogy* as a single film production, more than a decade after the original films, taking advantage of improvements in sound and visual technology, it grossed seventeen million dollars the first weekend. *The Phantom Menace*, which takes us back in time before the *Star Wars Trilogy* created such anticipation that movie-goers waited in line for hours to get tickets and then slept outside the theaters the night before the opening.

In December of 2015, Disney, who purchased the rights to *Star Wars* from Lucas, opened *The Force Awakens*. It takes place three decades after the defeat of the Galactic Empire with an aging Harrison Ford as Han Solo and an aging Carrie Fisher as Leia, now head of the Resistance against the first Order, searching for her twin, Luke Skywalker, who has disappeared. The movie grossed enough the first weekend to pay for it, $247 million, and it has grossed over $2 billion world-wide.

Primordial link to our human voyage

The attraction of the *Star Wars* story is its primordial link to our human voyage on our spaceship, to its re-enactment of our mythological quest for knowledge and understanding of how the power of the universe works and how the individual as one entity squares away a single life and fits into this paradigm. It is one man, capable of succeeding in the universe by trusting himself. Skywalker must defeat clearly defined evil, Darth Vadar. All the intention and mastery of the universe comes together in this moment of moral decision. Will it be the inhumanity and darkness of Darth Vadar, or will it be the victory of human purpose, of pure intention, of courageous action, the victory of heart?

"The Force"

When the voice of Ben Kenobi is heard by Skywalker at the crisis in the last battle, it says, "Turn off your computer, turn off your machine and do it yourself, follow your feelings, trust your feelings." Above, beyond any mechanism created by the human brain, the mind of man is linked with the One mind, and the One mind feels, has heart. Lucas calls it "The Force," defined as energy by Ben Kenobi: "The force is an energy field created by all living things. It surrounds us, it penetrates us, it binds the galaxy together." When Ben Kenobi says, "May *The Force* be with you," he is speaking of the power that binds together the hearts and mind and soul of humanity in a unified action of intention and integrity.

Humanity's united quest

The united quest of humanity on the planet is an expression of this force. It is what has led us to discover how things work, to move from being the product of an explosion to the creator of the explosion. It is the activity that has taken us from the observation of physical principles to the application of those principles metaphysically. It has empowered man to figure out that nothing in the universe exists except energy, that life itself and all matter in all of its expressions on our planet are nothing but energy: the plants, the rocks, the soil, the minerals, the ever-transforming water that covers two-thirds of the earth, constantly in flux between its form of vapor, liquid, and solid.

We have moved from the primitive man's wonder and fear of a flash of lightening in the sky, to the production of a spark by rubbing two sticks together, to the smashing of an atom to create a bomb of devastating destruction and a rocket powerful enough to thrust a space capsule of our fabrication outside the force of gravity that anchors our little planet and all of its passengers in orbit around the sun. Thus has man's voyage on his planet, his history as an astronaut, been spent in figuring out how his little spaceship works and how it fits within the universe it occupies.

Celestial ships: not just a dream

In perhaps the earliest work of science fiction, in the early 1600s, Johannes Kepler, about whom we will hear more in the chapter "Trial and Error," imagined the movement of our craft through space in *Somnium*, "The Dream." Since he knew that it was hard for people on earth to believe the earth was rotating because they didn't feel the movement, in his "dream" he imagines a journey to the moon with the space travelers observing Earth rotating above them. He imagines the continents and the oceans. He said of his dreaming, "…in a dream one must be allowed the liberty of imagining occasionally that which never existed in the world of sense perception." He believed one day there would be "celestial ships with sails adapted to the winds of heaven" navigating the sky, filled with explorers unafraid of the vastness of space.[3]

Explorers of an aged Universe

The 21st Century Hubble telescope has been refurbished; its value is estimated at $3.8 billion. It is anticipated that as the Hubble peers into the whirlpool of gas and dust swirling at the heart of the galaxy 100 million light years away, as it measures the velocity, decades of theoretical work on how objects interact to shape the cosmos may need to be eliminated or revised. We may find, for instance, that some of the oldest stars in the heavens, believed to be fifteen to twenty billion years old by our classic methods of measurement, may in fact be older than the universe itself.

Juno, which left earth in 2011, has just completed its initial journey and in 2016 joined in orbit around Jupiter. Juno carries instruments to measure and to calculate data revealing Jupiter's history and present. The scientists who designed Juno and sent it on its way are ecstatic, as they well should be, about their success. This is a celebration for mankind, for man's conquest of the unknown.

Time is our measurement, not the Universe's

Most of us do not wake up each morning wondering how old the universe is. If we have questions, they tend to concern themselves with ourselves. What we really want to know is where we stand with the universe, who we are, and where we are going. Should we have to modify our theories, it will not be the first time. Indeed, our natural process for sorting things out has been codified and defined as our scientific method: hypothesis, experiment, observation, conclusion. Man used this procedure long before we had a name for it. This is how we make discovery.

One theory will hold until we come up with another closer to the truth, closer to explaining the phenomena, the data we observe and analyze. We have grown enough in our under-standing to know our language is symbolic; it expresses our current truth, our present knowledge, explanation and com-prehension of the perfection of a machine that always works. Today we know it will be revised. It has not always been so.

'Tis so much joy! 'Tis so much joy!
If I should fail, what poverty!
And yet, as poor as I
Have ventured all upon a throw;
Have gained! Yes! Hesitated so
This side the victory!
Life is but life, and death but death!
Bliss is but bliss, and breath but breath!
And if, indeed, I fail,
At least to know the worst is sweet.
Defeat means nothing but defeat,
No drearier can prevail!
And if I gain, --oh, gun at sea,
Oh, bells that in the steeples be,
At first repeat if slow!
For heaven is a different thing
Conjecture, and waked sudden in,
And might o'erwhelm me so!

Emily Dickinson[1]

Our life is an apprenticeship to the truth that around every circle another can be drawn; that there is no end in nature, but every end is a beginning; that there is always another dawn risen on mid-noon and under every deep a lower deep opens.

Emerson, "Circles,"[2]

TRIAL AND ERROR

Man in center

WHEN THE LATE Carl Sagan's *Cosmos* series on public television was presented in the late 1970's, not only did it open the world of physics and scientific discovery to generally educated but non-scientific lay people, but also it put into perspective the absolutely devastating blow delivered to man's image of himself by Copernicus' message of truth about the movement of earth and the planets. When primitive man looked up in the sky, he assumed, as well he might, that the sky was out there, and he was at the center.

Ptomely's universe

It seemed only appropriate that Ptomely, the early astronomer who named the stars and made so many discoveries about them and their brightness, should corroborate man's central position. Ptomely observed that the Earth is a sphere, predicted eclipses, and established a model for plotting the movement of the planets. He concluded from his investigation of the heavens that the Earth was the center of the universe and that everything else moved around the Earth. This assumption nourished and sustained a religious belief based upon the premise that man, the child of God, is the center of the universe, and that all living and non-living things on the planet extend downward from him, and all angelical and heavenly things extend upward from him.

Copernicus: "upstart astrologer."

It is little wonder that when Nicholas Copernicus, in 1543, published a different hypothesis, reducing the earth to just another planet circling around the sun, he was met with indignation, denunciation and censorship. He had to be in error. How dare he undermine man's estimation of his place in the universe and the work of the philosophers, theologians, and poets who had celebrated it?

It was an outcry that would not die down. His "truth" was totally unacceptable. More than half a century after his discovery, in 1616, the Catholic Church put his work on a list of forbidden books. It stayed on that list until 1835. The denunciation was not limited to the Catholic Church. Martin Luther called Copernicus an "upstart astrologer."

When Johannes Kepler, born in 1571 in Germany, proved beyond a doubt that Copernicus' observation was sound, he softened the blow of his confirmation with this statement of understanding why the man-centered interpretation of the universe held power in man's explanation of his home for so many centuries: "It is therefore impossible that reason not pre-viously instructed should imagine anything other than that the Earth is a kind of vast house with the vault of the sky placed on top of it; it is motionless and without it the Sun being so small passes from one region to another, like a bird wandering through the air."[3]

God and geometry

Kepler observed the planets move according to precise mathematical laws and noted the time for a planet to complete one orbit is proportional to the cube of its distance from the sun, i.e. the farther from the sun, the more slowly it moves. He concluded from his work that God and Geometry were one: "Geometry existed before the Creation. It is co-eternal with the mind of God. Geometry provided God with a model for the Creation......Geometry is God himself."[4] Kepler even antic-ipated Newton and gravity by suggesting planetary movement was similar to the working of magnetism. He concluded the "celestial machine is to be likened not to a divine organism but rather to a clockwork. . . . insofar as nearly all the manifold movements are carried out by means of a single, quite sim-ple magnetic force, as in the case of a clockwork {where} all motions {are caused} by a single weight."[5]

God the clockmaker.

As Carl Sagan has observed, "Kepler stood at a cusp in his-tory; the last scientific astrologer was the first astrophysicist."[6] In his conception of God as a clockmaker, he demonstrates man's extraordinary ability to generalize from what is known, and to draw the conclusions from observations to take us to the next step in our understanding of the way things are. He proposed the same quantitative physical laws that apply to the Earth are also the quantitative physical laws governing the heavens, and he concluded, "Astronomy is part of physics."

Kepler knew the significance of this moment: "With this symphony of voices, man can play through the eternity of time in less than an hour, and can taste in small measure the delight of god, the supreme Artist. . . . I yield freely to the sacred frenzy. . . the die is cast, and I am writing the book – to be read either now or by posterity, it matters not. It can wait a century for a reader, as God himself has waited 6,000 years for a witness."[7]

Daddy not up there – then where?

The sixteenth-century "climate of opinion" and "race consciousness" did not take kindly to the reduction of God to a mathematician and to the analogy of God's work to making a clock. Kepler was excommunicated from the Lutheran church for his work because it disputed doctrine. His wife and son were wiped out by an epidemic; his mother in his hometown Weil der Stadt in Germany was accused of being a witch, chained and imprisoned in a Protestant dungeon.

The witch trials in this single community killed three witches a year between 1615 and 1629. In fact, the dates parallel our own Salem, Massachusetts witch trials. This is the great paradox, the great conundrum of human life, that the mind of man can comprehend so clearly, see so perfectly the mathematics of the workings of the Universe, and can be so enmeshed, so mired down in bias, prejudice, hysteria, and cruelty.

From the Cosmos to the Scapegoat

In Kepler's *Somnium*, in addition to imagining man in space travel, he tried to understand himself why he became such a scapegoat. He questioned why his life unfolded as it did, why there was so much religious persecution, why the fear of demons led people to torture his mother and women like her. Kepler's mind soared through the Universe, contemplated the cosmos, met God in Geometry, the clockmaker of planetary motion. Yet his body was trapped amidst the prejudices, fears, horrors, and sorrows of a race consciousness that has accompanied us on our journey since man's very beginning, The mindset we pass down generation to generation allows to mold and fester the dark side of us, the part that judges and condemns and hurts others. Kepler died outcast, without financial support. The oxen and the eagle, he composed his own epitaph: "I measured the skies, now the shadow I measure. Sky-bound was the mind, Earth-bound the body rests."[8]

Galileo imprisoned for telling truth

The earth-bound persecution for scientific discovery through observation did not end with Kepler. Indeed, it continued. Kepler died in 1630. In 1633 Galileo, the first astronomer to study the movement of the heavens with a telescope, was forced to stand trial by the Catholic hierarchy for "vehement suspicion of heresy." He spent the last eight years of his life under "house arrest" in his home near Florence.

Imagine the conversation!

Christophe Galfard's *The Universe in Your Hand: A Journey through Space, Time, and Beyond* was published in April of 2016.[10] Galford, a protégé of Stephen Hawking, holds a Ph.D. in theoretical physics from Cambridge University. He takes us on a voyage through theoretical physics and the quantum world with stories and metaphors that explain the theories that underpin everything we know about the universe.

Copernicus, Kepler, Newton, Galileo, Einstein, Heisenberg, Bohr all moved us forward on our way to the discoveries of the brilliant Nobel Prize winners of the twentieth and twenty-first centuries, to the Higgs Boson and the particle accelerator at the Centre for Nuclear Research near Geneva, Switzerland. Imagine if they could all sit down together. In Galfard's book they do. It is the most exciting book I have read in years, and I urge you to join Galfard in his "Journey."

If they did sit down together, there would be constant revision, testing of theories. As Carlo Rovelli documents in his *Seven Brief Lesson on Physics*, translated into English and published in the U.S. in 2016, the dialogues were continual, without end. Bohr and Einstein wrestled with the question of *probability* that goes to the heart of physics, "where everything had seemed to be regulated by firm laws that were universal and irrevocable."[11] Bohr would explain new ideas to Einstein, and Einstein would object: "For years, their dialogue continued by way of lectures, letters, articles. . .During the course of the exchange both great men needed to backtrack, to change their thinking. Einstein had to admit that there was actually no contradiction with the new ideas. Bohr had to recognize that things were not as simple and clear as he'd initially thought."[12]

Man's unique place in the great chain of being

As we noted earlier in the chapter "Man Is an Astronaut," man holds a unique place in the great chain of being of the universe. The creative mind, force, power, spirit that put this planet into place and action, pronounced *it* as done, and *it* was. The planet *is,* whether it came by way of a big bang or by way of Michelangelo's depiction on the ceiling of the Sistine Chapel. We, as human beings, are one stage in evolution of inhabitants here. But we are unique, unique in the place that we hold, for we learn by understanding through trial and error, communicate what we discover, and know by being understood.

Man's know-how

The lack of an operating manual for the planet forced us to develop our know-how. Primitive man ate white berries and then red berries and discovered that the red would nourish him and the white would kill him. The nature of the berries did not change. All that changed was our knowledge about the effect of the berries. As we evolved, we learned to cultivate the red berries that would nourish us. We may have even discovered a medicinal use for the white berries. The planets and the heavens did not change in their movement between the writing of Ptomely, Copernicus, and Kepler. All that changed was our understanding. The operation of the universe and of our planet is purposeful. Our human purpose is to discover what that purpose is and to use it effectively for our collective good.

The Bill and Melinda Gates Foundation, dedicated to eradicating disease on this planet, is not only developing the necessary treatment and vaccines. The "necessities" are driving invention. A thermal device that can keep vaccines cold for 50 days in hot climates has been invented. A toilet that will work without water has been invented. Each time we solve a problem, we make a discovery about how to make things work better.

Discovery through trial and error

We, the inhabitants of this universe and this planet, are assigned the task, by our very existence here, to figure things out, to discover that perfection of operation. The mechanical lessons in themselves just are. They have no emotion. We learn the mechanical lessons through trial and error. We generalize from what we discover, and we make new applications.

We named this process *the scientific method* long after we began to use it. Universe places no limit on this activity, for there is no limit to our thought. The issues are intensified, however, when these mechanical discoveries have generalized application. It affects how we think about our human condition; and it alters how we regard ourselves, how we interact, and how we interface with other people.

The time will come when diligent research over long periods will bring to light things which now lie hidden. A single lifetime, even though entirely devoted to the sky, would not be enough for the investigation of so vast a subject. . . . And so this knowledge will be unfolded only through long successive ages. There will come a time when our descendants will be amazed that we did not know things that are so plain to them. . . . Many discoveries are reserved for ages still to come, when memory of us will have been effaced. Our universe is a sorry little affair unless it has in it something for every age to investigate. . . . Nature does not reveal her mysteries once and for all.

Seneca, *Natural Questions*, Book VII

Into every intelligence there is a door, which is never closed, through which the creator passes. The intellect, seeker of absolute truth, or the heart, lover of absolute good, intervenes for our succor, and at one whisper of this high power we awake from ineffectual struggles with this nightmare.

Emerson, "Experience"[1]

THE METAPHYSICAL CONTEXT

Musty smell of discovery

WHAT FIRST ATTRACTED me to Fuller was his optimism, his belief in the absolute ability of the human mind and spirit to figure anything out. It was a consciousness of necessity, a belief that all discoveries are waiting to be made, that the Universal Mind put it all into action and is forever unfolding through us in our evolution. Part of this optimism was the belief everything in our universe works perfectly, has always worked perfectly. The only thing changed is our understanding of how it works. This means our knowledge grows exponentially, because the more we understand about the physical principles of the function of the universe, the more tools we have to pry open the next secret.

Physical and Metaphysical

Distinctions critical to the discussion are those between the physical and the metaphysical, between the brain and the mind. The physical is the observation of the principles of physical universe functioning. For instance, we use the physical principle of leverage to jack up our cars, to create levers and pulleys, to build dams and roads and bridges. In each instance we are doing more with less physical effort.

We take the same idea, the same way of doing something, or the same creative act, and we apply it beyond the physical. There is no limit to the metaphysical application. It moves outward in the realm of mind. Exchanges are made, mind to mind, thought to thought, and they are instantaneous. How long does it take to change one's mind? How long does it take to accept a thought? The mind moves in fractions of a second. The metaphysical application moves outward in physical production.

Leverage applied: physical to metaphysical

We use the metaphysical principle of leverage in our monetary system, in our mortgages to buy homes, where the down payment, the lever, lifts up the rest of the cost of the home. We use it when we write a single book and print a million copies; when we record a concert and sell 200,000 CD's; when we produce a single film and make $247 million the first weekend it's distributed, and then bring it out as a DVD sold all over the world.

There is no limit to how many copies can be made of a single performance of any activity. If we ever doubted that God meant us to live in an abundant universe, we have only to contemplate man's metaphysical application of physical law and physical creation. Universe, this perfect mind that put our perfect universe into existence, is forever giving. God is a great giver. Fuller believes that is the message conveyed by Jesus when he fed the multitude with five loaves and two fishes.

Brain and Mind

The brain

The distinction between brain and mind is also fundamental and definitely a part of the distinction between the physical and metaphysical. We know where the brain is located in the human body. We have surgeons who can go into the brain, who know the neurons and synapses, who can disconnect and re-connect. We have names for parts of the brain: the cortex, the frontal lobe, etc. We know the brain is lodged in the cranium of vertebrates, and every new discovery leaves us more in awe of its complexity.

The functions of the brain can be replicated. That is what the computer does. Just as the brain in us acts as a computer, so is the computer a replica of the human brain. The programmer breaks down into steps what the human brain performs automatically.

The mind

It is the mind, however, that conceived of the computer, for in the mind, as Robert Browning's Rabbi Ben Ezra discerns, "A whole I see." The mind *is*. The mind has no specific location. We know it as thought. Thought can come and go. Thought is both conscious and subconscious. We know thought by its action within us, through our awareness, through our perceptions. We can share our thoughts with others. We can't take our thoughts back. We know we can direct them and sort them. We can ignore negative thoughts and focus on positive thoughts.

Transformed by thoughts

We can change our thinking. We can look at events in our life; and through our thinking, we can re-interpret them. In our thoughts we can transform handicaps and deficiencies into challenges; we can regard personal loss and tragedy as opportunity for growth; we can re-construct an image of ourselves, of others, of our experience. There is the story of the pianist who was imprisoned and who practiced the piano every day in his mind. When he got out of prison, he performed a concert flawlessly even though he had not touched an actual piano in seven years.

Our inner genius by nature restored

When the mind of man is free from restraint, criticism, fear; when the mind of man is in balance, a recipient of the restorative power of nature, then he can best express his genius. We express our genius when, through comprehensive thinking, our mind links unlike elements, through some intuitive flash, making a connection, thereby discovering, or *rediscovering* how the universe works. Emerson, in "Spiritual Laws" observes man's genius:

> ...the quality that differences him from every other, the susceptibility to the one class of influences, the selection of what is fit for him, the rejection of what is unfit, determines for him the character of the universe. A man is a method, a progressive arrangement; a selection principle, gathering his like to him wherever he goes. He takes only his own out of the multiplicity that sweeps and circles round him.[2]

Our magnificent recollection

"Recall" is at the core of our human voyage on this planet, the action of mind over matter, the observation and discovery of the physical principles upon which universe operates, and the metaphysical application of those physical principles. In the great scheme of things, as we achieve understanding of the operation of the universe, we master the tools required to bring us into harmony with the underlying perfection of Universe's operation and the Mind responsible for its creation.

With this clarification of physical/metaphysical – mind/brain distinction, we are now ready to explore the concepts derived from observing how the planet works. As we do so, we will assume the "idea" that a perfect pattern underlies our experience. If it is muddled or misdirected, we have only to get clear and in touch, through our intuition and through our intellect, with that underlying perfection. The steps required to progress to the desired state will then be manifest.

Bill Clinton was playing golf with the Duke of York on Martha's Vineyard during his vacation. They were sitting in the golf cart, watching it rain. The Duke said, "I'll play you for the island. It used to be ours." Clinton replied, "Thank God it's raining!"

Earth
"A planet doesn't explode of itself," said drily
The Martian astronomer, gazing off into the air—
"That they were able to do it is proof that highly
Intelligent beings must have been living there."

John Hall Wheelock, 1961

A noiseless patient spider,
I mark'd where on a little promontory it stood isolated,
Mark'd how to explore the vacant vast surrounding,
It launch'd forth filament, filament, filament, out of itself,
Ever unreeling them, ever tirelessly speeding them.

And you O my soul where you stand,
Surrounded, detached in measureless oceans of space,
Ceaselessly musing, venturing, throwing, seeking the spheres to
   Connect them,
Till the bridge you will need be form'd, till the ductile anchor hold,
Till the gossamer thread you fling catch somewhere, O my soul.

Walt Whitman, 1862-63

The Red Wheelbarrow
so much depends

upon

a red wheel

barrow

glazed with rain

water

beside the white

chickens

William Carlos Williams 1923

PART 3: RESET

* **No Mistakes:**
  Only Opportunities to Discover the Truth

* **Piano Tops**

Midway along the journey of our life
  I woke to find myself in some dark woods,
  For I had wandered off from the straight path.

How hard it is to tell what it was like,
  This wood of wilderness, savage and stubborn
  (the thought of it brings back all my old fear),

A bitter place! Death could scarce be bitterer.
  But if I would show the good that came of it
  I must talk about things other than the good.

Dante, Inferno[1]

These roses under my window make no reference to former roses or to better ones; They are for what they are; they exist with God to-day. There is no time to them. There is simply the rose; it is perfect in every moment of its existence. Before a leaf-bud has burst, its whole life acts; in the full-blown flower there is no more; in the leafless root there is no less. Its nature is satisfied and it satisfies nature all in moments alike. But man postpones or remembers; he does not live in the present, but with reverted eye laments the past, or, heedless of the riches that surround him, stands on tiptoe to foresee the future.

Emerson, "Self Reliance"[2]

NO MISTAKES: ONLY OPPORTUNITIES TO DISCOVER THE TRUTH

Oedipus: The unconscious mistake

The tragic character

ARISTOTLE DEFINES THE tragic character as one who is basically good, but who, through excess, too much of a good thing, falls into error. Aristotle based his analysis of the perfect drama in his *Poetics* on the play, *Oedipus Rex,* by Sophocles. This play demonstrates the three unities: time, place, and action. The time is one twenty-four hour period; the place is outside the king's palace in Thebes; the action is Oedipus' discovery of his real identity, the truth about himself.

The city in plague

Oedipus is the most conscientious of kings. His city and his people are suffering from the siege of a plague. People are dying, sick, unable to work. No children are being born. He has come to speak directly to his people, not through emissaries: "I Oedipus whom all men call the Great."[3] He tells his people that he will get to the bottom of the cause of the plague; he will leave no stone unturned. He is the man you would want to lead your corporation, your organization, not isolated in his office surrounded by upper management, but out on the floor, zealous, curious and persistent.

The zealous search for truth

Oedipus has sent his brother-in-law, Creon, to consult with the oracle, Phoebus Apollo. Creon reports that Phoebus says he must find the murderer of the former king, Laius, whose wife, Jocasta, is now Oedipus' wife. Oedipus announces he will drive this person from the land. He calls Tiresias, the prophet. Tiresias does not want to speak, for he knows the truth Oedipus seeks. Oedipus gets angry, their tempers flare, and Tiresias, pushed to the wall tells him "You are the land's pollution!"[4] Oedipus, whose tragic flaw is often called *hubris*, self-pride, begins to call people in, each messenger bringing a fresh clue, each one uncovering the need for more information.

With dreadful irony, Sophocles contrasts the darkness and the light. Each discovery Oedipus makes, each fact he uncovers about apparent circumstances, each new bit of evidence illuminates and brings the truth closer to the light, leads Oedipus more deeply into the darkness of his own character. The awful truth is that Oedipus, on his way to Thebes, killed an old man at a crossroad where three roads meet. This was Laius. Oedipus did not know it was his father, for he believed himself to be the son of the King of Corinth. He is married to his mother, Jocasta. He has fathered three incestuous children. Jocasta hangs herself. Oedipus is the victim of the curse of the Gods on the House of Laius. Yet he fulfills the decree of exile he declared against the polluter of the land as the responsible and heroic man he is. Oedipus takes the brooch from Jocasta's dress and blinds himself, puts out his eyes. He leaves his city in self-exile.

The oracle fulfilled

This had all been foretold, that the son of Laius would murder his father and sleep with his mother. When Jocasta gave birth to a son, she was ordered by Laius, her husband and king, to abandon the child, the baby Oedipus, in the wilderness to die. Jocasta, instead, gave the child to a shepherd, who in turn gave the child to the king and queen of Corinth who raised him. When Oedipus, in adolescence, overheard that he had a curse upon him, that he was to murder his father and marry his mother, he ran away to avoid it, believing that the king and queen of Corinth were his real parents. He met Laius at a crossroad where three roads meet. Both had tempers, they got in a fight, and Oedipus killed Laius.. Oedipus then went on to Thebes where the sphinx held the city under siege. He solved the riddle of the sphinx: What walks on four legs in the morning, two at noon, and three at sundown? The answer is

"Man," who crawls as a child, stands upright at his prime, and walks with a cane in old age. Oedipus' reward was to marry the queen, Jocasta.

The Oedipus complex

Freud made this Oedipal situation the basis for the Oedipus complex. When Oedipus, in Sophocles' play, tells Jocasta about the curse he heard in Corinth, that he would kill his father and marry his mother, Jocasta sooths him by saying this is something men do in their dreams. Freud took Jocasta's words to define the Oedipus complex. Freud's psychoanalysis, rooted in the interpretation of dreams, as in the play, brings the buried darkness to light. The "collective unconscious" defined by Karl Jung is also in darkness. We bring it to light in order to understand ourselves. That which we shroud in darkness is error. We fear it. This is the emergence from the Dark of the Moon to the New Moon.

Fear of error: race consciousness.

The myth underlying the Oedipus story, the action of Sophocles' play, the basic tenet of Freud's psychoanalysis and Jung's collective unconscious, all have one thing in common, the human fear of being or acting in error. I consider it part of our race consciousness. In our western world, it is associated with the idea of sin. The word sinister has its roots in the Latin *sinstra*, meaning left. "Left" is the opposite of "right." It is good to be right handed; it is good to be right.

Error punished

It is wrong to be in error. We impart it to our children by demanding perfection. We punish them if they bring home papers from school marked up with red ink. We take away privileges. Mother put my bicycle in the garage. We may not even know we are sending the message so powerfully, may be delivering a sentence. My daughter, for instance, used to hide her report cards, wouldn't bring them home. If I asked, she would say she didn't get one. In retrospect, I realize her older brother's obsession for perfection, his pride in his report cards, and my praise of him for it, made her feel that if she had anything less than perfection, it wasn't good enough. I didn't mean to send that message, to sentence her in that way, not consciously. *But* I did.

All powerful "But"

But is the most powerful word in the English language. It eradicates all that went before it. Nothing eludes its power. The roses Emerson describes beneath his windows know no *but.* They are satisfied, perfect at every stage, at each unfoldment of their natural growth. There is nothing in the consciousness of a rose of right or wrong, good or evil. The rose just is. It knows no shame or guilt. It makes no apologies. People, on the other hand, beat themselves up because of error. They regret the past, mock the present, and fear the future. They hold up for themselves an image of perfection contrary to the natural principle of growth.

No truth without error

So here we are again with the paradox. Everything that we know about how our planet works was discovered by making mistakes. In the scientific method, a name applied to a process we developed pragmatically to test our hunches, the mistakes, the errors, the erroneously formulated conclusions, are absolutely essential to discovery of truth. It's like a swimmer doing the breast stroke, with each movement of the arms pushing away the dead weight of wrong answers in order to move forward to the right answer.

Doing, Discovering, and Discarding

When I was in kindergarten, someone told me, probably the boy next door, that I could make paste with flowers and water. So, I went out into the back yard, and I plucked the blossoms off from my mother's petunias. I chopped up the blossoms, added water, and then applied this fragrant paste to two pieces of paper. It didn't work. The papers came right apart. When mother came home and found her garden stripped of its flowers, she was not happy. I was equally distressed because my paste was not sticking. I explained to her that I was just trying to make paste. She informed me I had the wrong kind of *flower;* I needed to mix *flour* with water. What a blunder! So I quickly got some flour out of the cupboard, mixed it with water, and lo and behold, I made paste. It stuck.

Misdirection to mastery

As I look back on this experiment, I see that I learned not only a scientific lesson about adhesion, what makes things stick; but also I learned about the language, about words that sound alike but have different meanings, homonyms. It also is a lesson about how our actions are guided by words. Two infinitive phrases in the English language misdirect our thinking: "to try" and "to make mistakes." Nothing was ever accomplished by trying. We accomplish by doing. A mistake, by this way of thinking, is merely what we *mis* took as a truth. We cannot actually make mistakes; we can only temporarily misapprehend a truth, take something as a truth until we discover that it isn't and something else is. I think of it as three Ds: **Doing, Discovering**, and **Discarding**.

This is how we learn to cope and to master all aspects of living: to approach someone, to accomplish a task, to prepare a meal, to manufacture a product, to design a home, to drive a car, to ride a bicycle, to behave in a relationship, to overcome fear or anxiety, to express love, to deliver a lecture, to teach a class, to read a poem, to write a novel or screenplay, to wash a dog, to care for a baby. Our life is a continual process of practicing the three D's: **Doing, Discovering**, and **Discarding.**

Revising truth

We have come a long way in our acceptance of the process of discovery, i.e. uncovering error, and revision, i.e., revising what we see as true. We anticipate each day our research will bring us closer to understanding the way things work, but we know what is true today will inevitably be revised tomorrow. Take for instance, the human genome. For years companies and the National Institute of Health were racing to see who could decode it first. The genome has inscribed upon it all of the human genes, each gene causing one or more instruction. The genome is thus the full DNA tape, the operating manual for the cell, with 60,000 – 100,000 genes. In a recent "closed door "meeting, scientists presented evidence of the ability to create a human cell with preferred genes. The prospect of creating a "super" being presents ethical issues that will need to be addressed.

Today's truth: yesterday's mistake

The climate of opinion today accepts the idea that today's "truth" will be tomorrow's "mistake," something we *mis*-took as the truth, whether its the enzyme in the protein that causes Alzheimer's Disease or a vaccine against prostrate cancer or colon cancer. The more we know about the genetic basis for conditions, the more we discover about how the genes work, the better we will be able to eradicate disease, deformity, dysfunction.

We must stand in awe of our human ability to figure things out. We are in a whirlwind of discarding old ideas, former conclusions, and previous ways of solving problems. We anticipate each discovery will lead to future ones. We hold in esteem those uniquely endowed people who are at the forefront of scientific investigation, and we acknowledge the role of the computer in accelerating this process. How differently we think from the time of Copernicus and Galileo!

Bumps in the road

The progressive discovery, re-evaluation, rejection, and re-discovery of pure scientific truth is easier for us to deal with than that process unfolding within ourselves.

Our common vernacular has phrases for this: bumps in the road, dead ends, wrong turns, curves, off the beaten path, pitfalls along the way, off the map, off the chart, derailed. They all assume the right direction is going from point A to point B; and they all assume that, although there is a road to discovery, it is marked with error. Many of our most compelling human spiritual stories, stories we tell again and again for inspiration, have to do with a lost man who sees the light.

Down in the depths before the light

We must know the worst about ourselves before we are allowed to acknowledge the best about ourselves. This so often occurs allegorically along the road of life. The apostle, Paul, sees the light on the road from Tarsus. The poet, Dante, loses his way and ends up in the Dark Wood, the dark night of the soul, the "Dark of the Moon." His vision of the *Divine Comedy*, the progress of man's soul, follows it from eternal darkness in the inferno, through purgatory and into paradise. In the medieval *Piers the Plowman*, the dreamer, sees a vision of a high tower, Truth, and a deep dungeon, Wrong. The Seven Deadly

Sins, the carnal curse, must be purged before the pilgrim can seek St. Truth. In John Bunyan's *Pilgrim's Progress*, Christian flees the City of Destruction and begins his pilgrimage to the Celestial city. Among his many stops and encounters along the way, he passes through the Slough of Despond, the Valley of Humiliation, and the Valley of the Shadow of Death. Finally, the Giant Despair must be overcome before he may have his beatific vision. Gerard Manley Hopkins, the converted Catholic priest who found his parish assignment in Ireland such a trial, proclaims in one of his sonnets written during a period of despair, "Oh the mind, mind has mountains, / Cliffs of Fall. / Hold them lightly he who has never been there."

No winner without a loser

The scientific method demands mistakes. The psychological, social, emotional judgment that we apply to ourselves when we make mistakes, comes from a race consciousness demanding error-proof performance. It reminds me of the ambiguity of my own self-absorbed sentence. We want our children to compete, yet in every competition it is inevitable there will be a winner and a loser. We tell them to be "good losers," but we also let them know by the other 93% of our communication that "nobody loves a loser."

Mistakes: a psychological impulse

The "Business" news in any newspaper is a continual exposure of error, fraud, manipulation of the truth. Why is the public so easily misled? There are more ways than ever to research, monitor and manage your finances, whether through discount brokers, a flood of financial publications, constant television coverage or the Internet. But though the investing world may have changed, people haven't; our errors remain remarkably similar. That's because the psychological impulses behind many of our mistakes remain the same. How often do we say: "It sounds too good to be true." And then we ignore our own words.

I recall a scandal involving an Orange County California. investment group that claimed to be involved in the film industry and offered programs yielding 24% a year.

They had a compelling story: The founder of the firm was Sicilian, had ties in Sicily, owned a bank in Sicily, and could assist in off-shore banking and tax sheltering, i.e. evasion. Their investors included eminent sports figures, Hollywood stars, and high-flying corporate investors. When the court appointed an investigative team, they discovered the officers of the firm had shared a jail cell, the company was incorporated under the name of a chauffeur who didn't even know it, the "Sicilian" had no old-world ties, and apparently none of the money placed with them for investment had gone into investments, but rather had been spent to support luxuriously lavish life-styles for members of the firm - multi-million dollar homes, fleets of expensive cars, Nordstrom shopping, extravagant travel. Lured by the high yield, working people had moved their entire retirement funds into this company, often convinced by relatives whom they considered to be savvy investors. Too good to be true!

The 2016 Academy Award winning *The Big Short* tells the story of the sub-prime mortgage crisis that caused the Recession of 2008 from the standpoint of the banking insiders. It doesn't focus on the people who flocked to the banks to buy houses they couldn't afford, who failed to read the small print about the adjustable mortgages, and who ended up in eviction from foreclosure. These turned out to be enormous "mis"takes. and we are still in economic recovery from it.

To err is human

Yes, "to err is human." The rest of the passage reads, "To forgive, divine." The hardest person to forgive: one's self. Where do we make mistakes? In our relationships, our health choices, our jobs, our money. At least 50% of marriages end up in divorce. A physician recommends surgery, the procedure leads to complications, and you end up with a staph infection contracted in the hospital. The plastic surgeon sews your face back on crooked. You take a job and discover the boss is a tyrant and your colleagues duplicitous. You take out student loans to train for a profession replaced by automation and you can't find work. In every instance where we made a "mis"take, we have explanations for making the decisions, whether faulty intellectual analysis, bad judgment, psychological impulse, emotional infatuation. We each have a list!

Fear and shame

Even when we say we learned from the mistakes, we are left more fearful, less aggressive, less certain. Fear walks hand in hand with shame. Guilt is something we may feel bad about inside for an error we made. The guilt we can own alone. Shame is public: "What will people say, what will people think?" It is hard to admit we made mistakes because we feel ashamed. If I were to ask you how many times you've arrived at your destination on time and without problems, you probably would be challenged to report. If I were to ask you how many times you've been lost and the circumstances, you could probably account for every one. If I were to ask you what you did "right" yesterday, you probably would be a while in putting together the inventory. If I were to ask you what you did "wrong," yesterday, what "mistakes" you made, you would have them right at the tip of your tongue, readily available in your conscious mind. You may have revisited those mistakes several times today already, and you may even have rehearsed how you might have altered and reversed the situation.

We can't learn less

When we put our energy into our errors, they are magnified out of proportion; and we then lack the energy to focus on the positive. We learn by trial and error. Mistakes are positive. The PBS special on R. Buckminster Fuller's life shows the footage of the collapse of the first geodesic dome he built at Black Mountain in North Carolina. One of his associates there that summer, who heard the great "whoosh" as it came tumbling down, said she felt heartbroken for him. But Fuller, undaunted, just observed that he never expected it to stay up, that he learned from seeing it fall down, that he learned through failure. Fuller tells us, "We cannot change one iota of yesterday." He also observes:

> ...Every time man makes a new experiment he always learns more. He cannot learn less. He may learn that what he thought was true was not true. By the elimination of a false premise, his basic capital wealth is disembarrassed of further preoccupation with considerations of how to employ a worthless time-consuming hypothesis.... Every time we employ and test our intellectual know-how by experimental re-arrangement of physical energy inter-actions...we always learn more. The know-how can only increase.[5]

Every *mis*take is an opportunity to discover the truth. You can not change one iota of yesterday. Release it. This will free you to be fully present in the present. Just as the roses under Emerson's window make no apologies, neither should you.

"The changes which break up at short intervals the prosperity of men are advertisements of a nature whose law is growth. Every soul is by this intrinsic necessity quitting its whole system of things, its friends and home and laws and faith, as the shell-fish crawls out of its beautiful but stony case, because it no longer admits of its growth, and slowly forms a new house."

Emerson, "Compensation"[1]

PIANO TOPS

The Tiger and the Goats

Giving birth

AN ANCIENT ANIMAL fable, one the late mythologist, Joseph Campbell, tells again and again, is the story about a female tiger and her unborn son. The mother is pregnant, just about to deliver, and for various reasons has been without food for several days. She is absolutely starving. She comes out of the jungle onto a grassy meadow, and there right in front of her, she sees a herd of goats eating grass. She thinks to her self, "Ah ha! Here is what I need." Her heart starts to beat, the adrenalin courses through her burdensome body, and with great fervor, she pounces upon the goat closest to her. She gives it all of the force she has left, and in the strenuous act gives birth to a baby tiger and dies.

Adopted baby

The frightened goats all scatter, but when they realize that the imminent danger has passed, that the drama has ceased, they come back to the scene of attack. There they find the dead mother tiger and the baby tiger. Now goats are givers of milk, they are great nurturers, and they have great parental instincts. It goes against their nature to abandon the little baby tiger to predators like his mother, so they adopt him. One of the mother goats nurses the little tiger until he is strong and mature enough to have real food. They raise him as one of themselves, as a goat. He learns to eat grass and to bleat. As he approaches adolescence, he has a slightly confused demeanor, but most adolescents do, and no one in the herd thinks much about it.

The big male tiger and the baby

One day an enormous male tiger, very hungry, comes upon the herd of goats, and all of the goats scatter. But the little tiger, because he is a tiger and not a goat, stays.

The big fellow looks at the little fellow, and he says, "What are you doing here with these goats? You're a tiger."

And the little fellow looks at him, says, "Baaah," and takes a little nibble of grass.

The big fellow thinks what to do next, so he decides to give the little tiger a visual lesson. He takes the neck of the little tiger in his mouth and carries him to a pond, totally still, and sets the little fellow down where he can see himself.

"Now," he says, "Just look at you. You aren't a goat. You're a tiger."

The little fellow looks, says, "Baaah," and takes another nibble of grass.

The big fellow can't stand this grazing and Baahing, so he says to himself,

"What I need to do is to get this little tiger out of this meadow."

The little tiger's tigerness

He picks the little one up by the neck again and carries him off to his den. Strewn all over his den are the remains of the gazelle he had just killed and eaten. They are lying all around, and the smell of the fresh blood from the kill nauseates the little fellow.

"Here," the big male tiger says to the little fellow, offering him a big, bloody chunk, "Have some."

The little fellow says, "Baah, I'm a vegetarian."

Now this big male tiger is getting more than a bit impatient with this sassy little sissy. So he says, "You are a tiger, and tigers eat gazelles." And he grabs a hunk of gazelle meal and forces the chunk down the little fellow's throat.

The digestion of the gazelle meat warms the innards of the little fellow. He feels a power and vitality moving though his body as he awakens to instincts within himself, long dormant. His blood begins to flow, and he feels fire and passion, feelings he never had before. He lets out his first, little tiger roar. It feels so good, he does it again, only louder and more powerful.

"Now," says the big fellow, "You are a tiger. Go into the forest and be who you are."

Mistaken identity

It is obvious from this story that all along this little fellow was a tiger among goats. He just didn't know it. His hanging out with goats had nothing to do with his actual tigerness. At the appropriate opportunity, with the right leadership, he saw who he really was. The tiger had been there all the time and was ready to express itself. Just as John Cotton, Viscount of Greystoke, was there all the time when he was being raised as Tarzan by Kala, his ape mother.

Temporary life-savers

R. Buckminster Fuller opens *Operating Manual for Spaceship Earth* with this statement: "If you are in a shipwreck and all the boats are gone, a piano top buoyant enough to keep you afloat that comes along makes a fortuitous life preserver. This is not to say that the best way to design a life preserver is in the form of a piano top. I think that we are clinging to a great many piano tops in accepting yesterday's fortuitous contrivings as constituting the only means for solving a given problem."[2]

Goat Mother: Tiger's Piano Top

What a blessing it was for the baby tiger to be saved by the mother goat!

It would never have occurred to him that his living situation did not support the expression of his true identity. He was comfortable, accepted, within his adopted community. Had the hungry male tiger not invaded the flock of goats, the "baby" tiger might never have known his true nature. We, looking in, can see that the mother goat and the flock of goats were a temporary lifesaver, a "piano top," but the "baby" tiger might never have known it for himself.

This dichotomy between inner and outer evaluation and discernment prevails.

Just look around you and listen. It is relatively easy to identify the "piano tops" clutched by the institutions in our culture. We observe humanity clinging to a great many piano tops that were meant to be temporary solutions; and, indeed, in many cases we have come close to institutionalizing the piano top. As a nation we see it in our defense, in our education, in our government. It is more of a challenge, one requiring introspection and detachment, to see it in our personal lives, in our relationships, in our jobs, in our methods of confronting obstacles.

United Nations: Dysfunctional Piano Top

Whatever optimism might have been generated about planetary disarmament by the dismantling of the Berlin Wall was certainly eradicated by the invasion of Iraq on the grounds of weapons of mass destruction. We recognize world peace has not come, and the best apparent deterrent to war is still preparation for war. Instead of nuclear weapons in the hands of two nations, now they are spread out among both the developed and the undeveloped. The nations are too unpredictable.

The U.S. has invested years in wars in Iraq and Afghanistan that we find difficult to comprehend politically and even less the enormous cost in people and treasure. The U.S. pulled out of Iraq only to see the territories and cities we freed to be claimed by Isis. They even confiscated the weapons and vehicles we left behind. The Middle East is wracked with Civil uprisings. The Arab Spring is a nightmare of the first order as nations ill-equipped for democracy are torn between factions and vulnerable to invasion and control by Isis. The Sunni's and Shiites are at each other's throats in Iraq. Iran, with the assistance of Russia, feeds the fire. Russia supports tyranny in Syria's Civil War, and millions of Syrian refugees flood Europe. China's Coast Guard has moved into the South China Sea, and China has constructed an island off the coast of the Philippines. This is a threat to Japan, Viet Nam, and the Philippines.

The extreme hatred of the United States that prompted destruction of the two towers of the World Trade Center continues to thrive. Young Jihadists migrate to Syria, to Yemen, to strategic centers in Europe. We seem to be living with a cauldron of rage that could erupt at any moment. If ever an organization functioned as a "Piano Top," it is the United Nations.

The United States: planetary policeman

Although we would like to believe we can sit down at the table, man to man, woman to woman, and hammer out an agreement that works, one acceptable to both sides, alas, there are many sides; and human beings generally fail to come to agreement, even for their own families, let alone for the planet. We presently have enough nuclear weapons in existence on the planet to blow it up seventeen times. No one really believes the agreement with Iran will keep them from building a nuclear bomb. So if the planet still needs to be policed, a prevailing "Piano Top," I, for one, prefer the police action of the United States over any other. I say this with deep regret, having been one of those in the '80s blaring out "We Are the World, We Are the Children." We still are.

Education deteriorated

The state of our education is equally discouraging. Great deterioration occurred when school systems started grabbing on to piano tops to improve the pedagogical methods of teachers: Whole word reading system, new math, bilingual education, Common Core. Schools in the United States are producing graduates who are illiterate, the "dumbing of America." How did it come to be? For one thing, we have ignored the basics. My grandmother, with an eighth grade education in a one-room schoolhouse, was better educated than most high school graduates and even many college graduates.

Reading

Our children cannot read. Schools in California are just now returning to phonics after losing a decade of students with the whole word reading system. This return to phonics presents us with another unanticipated problem, a generation of teachers who themselves never learned phonics, who have to be re-educated in order to teach the basics. This is not an issue of money. The city of Inglewood, at the bottom of the economic hierarchy, has managed to achieve higher scores on standardized tests than Beverly Hills, just by returning to basic phonics.

Math

Our students cannot do basic math. Asian immigrant students find college-level math classes easy. Why? They mastered the rudiments in elementary school and high school. Here memorizing the multiplication tables was abandoned for calculators. The graduates of high school are so dependent upon calculators they can't perform simple problems in their heads, can't even make change when the cash register computer is down. When we grabbed on to calculators as lifesavers, we forgot they were originally programmed by human beings who told them what to do. We need to put more emphasis on memorization, on honing and perfecting the capacity of the original computer, our human brain.

Bilingual education

Our immigrant students are confused. The immigrants who came to the United States in the eighteenth and nineteenth century abandoned their old language and learned English. It was their ticket to success in their adopted land. We thought in the last half of the twentieth century that we could improve the performance of immigrants by teaching them first in their native tongue. It didn't work. We've returned to immersion.

Quick fixes

Nothing improved by grabbing on to these piano tops. Common Core has not solved our education problems. Teachers teach to the tests We have a nation with skewed values. Young people preparing for a teaching career are discouraged because "there's no money in that," yet athletes are paid millions of dollars for chasing after a ball. When we put the money into our schools, often the administration takes care of itself, and the funds never make their way into classroom instruction and teacher support. There is an enormous gap between the intent of the people and the implementation of the bureaucracy.

Governmental dysfunction: flagrant Piano Top

Since attorneys have the greatest facility with the language, spend years learning to manipulate the truth, and practice delivery of deception with sincerity, it evolved that they began to "run" for public office and then made an institution of it. We long ago left behind the farmers, the merchants, and the makers who came together to frame the Constitution of the United States. For them public service was a duty they would accept for a short term to serve their nation, an inconvenience they would tolerate in exchange for the exercise of the right of freedom.

Masters of deception indebted to special interests

We elect and re-elect to public office self-made masters of deception. Then we complain that our problems are not being solved. We put people in a position to make decisions about finance, agriculture, building projects, health care, and industry who have never met a payroll, never constructed a building, never built a road, never treated a patient, never invented nor manufactured anything. They are influenced in their decisions by the lobbyists who mold them and make them, and by big-money corporate backers who fund their campaigns.

Institutional practices replicated in personal choices

When we examine the institutionalized piano tops that we accept as normal and seldom question, it's little wonder we each do the same thing in our personal lives. We cling to jobs, to relationships, to organizations, to systems of belief, long after they have ceased to serve us. Why do we do this? Often it is inertia. Change requires too much energy. Often it is fear, fear that if we let go of the piano top, the better lifesaver or the real lifesaver may not show up. So long as we cling to the old piano top, there's no space for the real thing. Thus, the trap is set.

Trap distinguished from solution

How can we distinguish a trap from a solution or an opportunity? A trap creates the same results over and over without ever solving the problem and without space for growth and change: the hamster wheel. How do we get out of the trap? Open the trap door. Where is this trap door? It's in our minds, in our thoughts. We may think it's in our wallets and purses, in our beds or on our kitchen tables, or in the restaurant where we eat breakfast every morning; but it's in our thinking. Emerson claims "There is a crack in everything God has made." That means we still have a chance.

Reality determined by thought

I recall showing a home to a gentleman with knee problems who wanted to sell his tri-level home and move to a single story home. For several years he had been confined to a few rooms in his house because he couldn't go up and down the stairs. The home we visited was in a quiet, well-kept neighborhood behind a code-operated gate. The owner was a fastidious housekeeper and creative decorator, so it was attractive and inviting. The gentleman liked the home, in fact, wanted to know if the owner would sell the furniture because he acknowledged he could never decorate so effectively on his own.

Then began his doubts and fears.

Buyer: How can my friends drop in to visit me?

Realtor: Oh, just give them the code to the gate. Do your friends usually drop over without calling first?

Buyer: Well, actually hardly anyone just drops by. Besides, my friends won't feel comfortable in such a nice house.

Realtor: Will you feel at home in this house?

Buyer: I've never lived in such a nice house.

Realtor: This is a small neighborhood, and the people get along well. You probably would make some new friends.

Buyer: Actually, I've been alone for a long time. I don't really have many friends.

Vulnerability of the unknown

No decision a decision

The cost of this home was not an issue, because this gentleman's present home, which he inhabited only partially, finally sold for more than this one. He liked this house, yet articulated a fear that if he let go of his current way of living, he would lose his friendships. In the end, the friendships weren't the issue. The house represented to him a new way of life, a new kind of being, a new self-image. To move there would leave him open to the unknown, and he would relinquish his comfort zone. This is vulnerability. The choice of a home is emotional, and making that choice is a kind of exposure. The buyer resolved the problem. He didn't make a decision. Someone else put in an offer the same day and got the house. No decision is a decision.

Hanging On

We hang on to piano tops because we fear vulnerability, we fear any change in the *status quo*; and we prefer inertia to decisiveness. Events force change. During the first half of the 1990's, after Gorbachev took down a symbolic piano top, the Berlin Wall, the State of California was in disarray. For almost half a century we had created a defense mythos based on what the Berlin Wall was walling in: The Soviet Union, the giant monster with its missiles aimed at the U.S. A major portion of the U.S. defense industry operation was located in California. When the wall came down, it was apparent to the general public that the Soviet Union was weaker than we had believed, that Communism had failed, that an idea more than a reality had dominated our U.S. budget and defense spending. A cartoon read, "Will the last Communist please turn out the lights." We might even have reason to suspect that our lawyer-run government took advantage of the wall to mobilize our defense spending and to keep the economy rolling.

Sudden loss

When that same government acted in sudden haste to cut defense spending, without the foresight to re-direct that spending to the multitude of domestic problems needing solutions, many of the best-trained aerospace engineers in the world were put out of work. Along with them went their support personnel. This decision affected everyone in California: builders, bankers, grocers, dry cleaners, car salesmen, mechanics, retailers, realtors, clergymen, psychologists, educators. Those who provided homes, things, food, and toys lost or went out of business. Those who provided helping services picked up. This was true especially for education. The same cataclysmic chain of events accompanied the crash of 2008, not just in California, but also across the United States.

Education in bad economy

When the economy is bad, people go back to school. The upside: loss of jobs frees displaced and downsized workers to explore aspects of themselves they had stifled in their previous work, the work they did to make ends meet. Those who survived after displacement in the 1990's became teachers, counselors, entrepreneurs. In many cases, they were much happier. I particularly recall one gentleman who had built missiles for Rockwell. Although he disliked his work, he was trapped by his income. His true love was coaching, which he had done on the side. He used this opportunity to get a teaching credential, to follow his heart. His greatest worry, whether his daughter would be able to go to college, was eliminated by his loss of income. She qualified for a scholarship.

Forced renewal

The Recession of 2008 was more devastating with less upside. The forced vulnerability from the downsizing, the social euphemism for getting fired, was cataclysmic. Most spent the first six months to a year in depression, guilt, and fear, paralyzed by the shock of the event. Homes were lost, cars were lost, children were forced to drop out of college. Everyone in the family took a hit. Family members started to lay blame, to get angry and hostile. Divorces occurred. The forced renewal, reconstruction, rediscovery was at great price. Emerson sums it up with this observation:

> Our strength grows out of our weakness. The indignation which arms itself with secret forces does not awaken until we are pricked and stung and sorely assailed. A great man is always willing to be little. Whilst he sits on the cushion of advantages, he goes to sleep. When he is pushed, tormented, defeated, he has a chance to learn something; he has been put on his wits, on his manhood; he has gained facts; learns his ignorance; is cured of the insanity of conceit; has got moderation and real skill.[3]

It takes courage to let go of comfort and security, even if what you are doing isn't using your talents and abilities. Those without a lifesaver, a lifeline, would have given anything for a piano top. Out of fear of the unknown, we stay attached to a piano top long after it ceases to meet our challenges or to reward us financially.

Gone fishing!

Unemployment subsidy is a piano top. Welfare payments are a piano top. We need creative solutions. Fuller advocates replacing unemployment with fishing fellowships. He would "give each human who is or becomes unemployed a life fellowship in research development or in just simple thinking. Man must be able to dare to think truthfully and to act accordingly without fear of losing his franchise to live."[4] By his calculation, if we had 100,000 people on Fishing Fellowships, that is just fishing and thinking, one brilliant idea would generate enough income to pay for the 99,999 other fellowships.

Indecision: seedling of fear

Fear holds us back from truly knowing who we are or what we can do. When we are afraid, our intuition gets blocked and can't get through to us. Napoleon Hill regards indecision, doubt, and fear as a package: "Indecision is the seedling of fear!... Indecision crystallizes into doubt, the two blend and become fear! The blending process often is slow. This is one reason why these three enemies are so dangerous. They germinate and grow *without their presence being observed*."[5] The concept of a piano top is a vehicle for moving beyond that fear to take action.

Relationships: emotionally charged vulnerability

When we come to the primary relationships in our lives, we are dealing with issues that may seem over-simplified by a symbolic "piano top." That is, however, precisely why the concept works so effectively. It isn't emotionally charged; it is neutral. When we examine a relationship, directly, head-on, we get sidetracked by our feelings or by a sense of obligation. Always with a piano top we are asking, "Is this a permanent solution or is it a temporary life-saver?"

Stuck in the condition

Once a piano top is defined, we can ask the right questions. It facilitates the process of "letting go" or "getting out of" a relationship that has become a trap, chaining us to the hamster wheel. The trap is particularly powerful when the relationship fits definitions addressed in support groups and by 12-step programs, for instance co-dependence or victimization. I am not denigrating the work of such programs. I do, however, observe they focus on the condition. When all we can think about is the condition and how it affects our life, it is very difficult to think beyond it and to free our thought to find a solution, or to find a better way to live and love. When we look at our life from inside the problem we've labeled, we get stuck in the condition and can't get far enough away to ask the important question, "Is this working for my greatest good?"

Separate and neutral

One of my clients, for instance, was in a relationship with a woman who borrowed money from him, always with excuses of losing her job or getting sick or helping her family. He finally discovered she had a drug addiction problem, and she was using the money for cocaine. Another client discovered her boyfriend of seven years, to whom she considered herself "engaged," had been cheating on her with another woman for the past three years.   Both realized the relationship was a piano top. The "piano top" concept worked for them precisely because of its separation and neutrality, its freedom from outcomes. A mature, lasting, loving relationship must have an inner integrity to support and sustain it. Each of these people, by asking the hard question, was able to see the callous deception, use, and abuse practiced by the partner totally obliterated any possibility for such integrity. It was obvious that to continue to cling to the relationship for any reason was wasting time and resources.

The hard questions

We get clear, unmuddled answers when we ask the hard questions. Is this a rewarding situation? Or has a temporary lifesaver been adopted permanently through habit, or neglect, or fear that I'm just not good enough for something better? The definition of insanity is doing the things we've always done expecting different results, the hamster wheel. Knowledge is power. When we ask ourselves these basic questions about our work, about our friends, about our affiliations, about our primary relationships, we can get clear.

Push the *reset* button

Suppose you ask, "Does this relationship/job/organization energize me, inspire me, ignite me, invigorate me, empower me?" It is not working if the response is: "It boxes me in, subdues me, stifles me, suppresses me. " It's a piano top. I encourage you to engage in self-examination to help you determine where you are self-sufficient and where you are attached, where you are free and where you are trapped. Remember, there is a difference between dependence and symbiosis. In dependency one side clings to the other and cannot sustain itself alone. In symbiosis, both sides can function independently, but they come together for mutual advantage. They function more successfully together than apart. This term has biological roots referring to two species of organisms, such as a fungus and alga, which together make a lichen.

Piano top conversion

Don't expect perfect clarity, black and white. The subtle ambiguity of life makes it interesting. You will probably discover there are elements of empowerment and elements of suppression in your relationships. This does not mean that you need to throw out the baby with the bath. It may mean that you need to examine what serves you and what doesn't, and then to ask how it could change. In other words, you may be able to convert a piano top to a workable model of a lifesaver with just a few modifications, perhaps with something so simple as an earnest and sincere conversation with your significant other or your boss.

You are invited to examine the main categories of your life; people, institutions and things. *People* may include your primary relationship, your parents or siblings, your children, your friends, your colleagues or associates, your employer. *Institutions* may be the company you work for, your church, your school, your service clubs or affiliate organizations. *Things* may be food or drink, toys, or activities. Include sources of recreation and revitalization under *things*.

Choice verbs and adjectives

In each instance, ask yourself, how does this serve me? What are the ways it could improve? Here are some adjectives you may find useful to add to your own list: empowered, supported, reinforced, energized, encouraged, inhibited, reserved, stymied, confined, trapped. Notice that each of these adjectives is derived from a verb. The more we verb our life, the more vital it becomes. The verbs significantly define our actions or ways of being: to be, to know, to feel, to give, to take, to accept, to love, to engender, to create, to investigate, to determine, to go, to come, to consider, to fear, to believe.

PART 4: REBOOT

* **BIG PICTURE**

* **TRUE WEALTH**

He is entered in the universe even to our fingernail-tips, like a razor in a razorcase or fire in firewood. Him those people see not, for as seen, he is incomplete. When breathing, he becomes 'breath' by name; when speaking, 'voice'; when seeing, 'the eye'; when hearing, 'the ear'; when thinking, 'mind': these are but the names of his acts. Whoever worships one or another of these - knows not; for he is incomplete in one or another of these.

One should worship with the thought that he is one's self, for therein all these become one. This Self is the footprint of that All, for by it one knows the All – just as, verily, by following a footprint one finds cattle that have been lost.

Brihaderanyaka Upanishad 1.4.5 and 7 [1]

Character is this moral order seen through the medium of an individual nature. An individual is an encloser. Time and space, liberty and necessity, truth and thought are left at large no longer. . . . He animates all he can, and he sees only what he animates. He encloses the world, as the patriot does his country, as a material basis for his character, and a theatre for action. A healthy soul stands united with the Just and the True, as the magnet arranges itself with the pole; so that he stands to all beholders like a transparent object betwixt them and the sun, and whoso journeys toward the sun, journeys towards that person. He is thus the medium of the highest influence to all who are not on the same level. Thus men of character are the conscience of the society to which they belong.

Emerson, "Character" [2]

BIG PICTURE

Reset and Reboot?

I'VE BEEN TOLD that "reset" and "reboot" are the same thing. What is my distinction? For one thing, we "reset" small things like hair dryers and garbage disposals. We "reboot" the computers that essentially control our lives. Without them, we are immobilized. It is one thing to forgive ourselves for our focus on past errors, mistakes, or our dependence on illusions of stability, piano tops. It is quite another thing to recreate our vision of what can be and to re-assess our capacity to achieve that vision. After forgiveness and release, we can move on to the larger issue, remolding and remaking. This is what the section on "Reboot" is about. You are going to be invited to envision the "Big Picture" for your life and to assess your enormous capacity to achieve it, your "True Wealth." Once again, I turn to my literary touchstones.

To the Lighthouse: A "Big Picture" of achievement

If the weather is fine

The central issue in Virginia Woolf's *To the Lighthouse* is achievement, symbolized by reaching the Lighthouse. It becomes the "big picture" for several members of the Ramsay family and one of their guests, all assembled at the Ramsay's summer home at the shore in England. It begins with talk of the weather, "If it's fine tomorrow." The conflict in the plot is the life choice represented by the two parents, Mr. and Mrs. Ramsay. Mrs. Ramsay wants everything to stay just as it is, frozen in time, warm, comforting. Mr. Ramsay wants only the truth and will follow wherever it leads him. Mrs. Ramsay is soft and round, like a lap to sit in. Mr. Ramsay is hard and linear, like a remote Lighthouse on a rugged promontory. The son, James, is caught in the middle. James, only six, takes his mother's comment, "If it's fine tomorrow," as a promise that his dream of going to the Lighthouse will, indeed, be realized:

> To her son these words conveyed an extraordinary joy,
> as if it were settled, the expedition were bound to take
> place, and the wonder to which he had looked forward,
> for years and years it seemed, was, after a night's dark-
> ness and a day's sail, within touch. Since he belonged,
> even at the age of six, to that great clan which cannot
> keep this feeling separate from that, but must let future
> prospects, with their joys and sorrows, cloud what is
> actually at hand since to such people even in earliest

childhood any turn in the wheel of sensation has the power to crystallize and transfix the moment upon which its gloom or radiance rests. . . [3]

But: not fine.

Then James' father, Mr. Ramsay, swoops down upon them and declares, "But it won't be fine." There it is, that *but*, the most powerful word in the English language: "Had there been an axe handy, or a poker, any weapon that would have gashed a hole in his father's breast and killed him, there and then, James would have seized it. Such were the extremes of emotion that Mr. Ramsay excited in his children's breasts by his mere presence."[4] James is caught between his intuitive, loving, ingratiating, exaggerating mother, who wants everyone to be comfortable and cozy and harmonious and hopeful; and his ramrod father, truth telling, domineering, stern: "He was incapable of untruth; never tampered with a fact; never altered a disagreeable word to suit the pleasure or convenience of any mortal being, least of all of his own children. . . ." [5]

Caught in the middle: the dilemma

To stay with the known, the warm and cozy, or to go with the unknown, to be tested, that is the question, the dilemma. The entire household, the eight Ramsay children, the houseguests, all are immobilized, caught between the comfort of Mrs. Ramsay's beauty and charm and the cold, hard, bright light of truth represented by Mr. Ramsay and by the Lighthouse. Mr.

Ramsay, a philosopher, attempting to put all thought in order A to Z, has never been able to get beyond "Q" in his thinking. One guest in particular, Lily Briscoe, a maiden lady, is painting a picture which she can't get quite right. What holds her back? Her painting is an act of *self-assertion*, a frightening thing, against all that is honored in the present "climate of opinion." Charles Tansley, another houseguest, taunts her by muttering, "Women can't paint, women can't write." As for Mrs. Ramsay, Lily can only acknowledge the awful truth parenthetically, "(but Mrs. Ramsay cared not a fig for her painting)". [6] Lily is paralyzed by her own thinking.

Mrs. Ramsay: the comfort of the status quo

Mrs. Ramsay is a potent force on everyone's thinking; for she dominates and determines the climate of opinion. Mrs. Ramsay, who never wants her children to grow up, who knows they will "never be so happy again," dislikes the things said about her, "wishing to dominate, wishing to interfere, making people do what she wished – that was the charge against her and she thought it most unjust." It's just that when she looks at life, "a sort of transaction went on between them, in which she was on one side, and life was on another, and she was always trying to get the better of it, as it was of her. . . . for that reason, knowing what was before them – love and ambition and being wretched alone in dreary places – she had often the feeling, 'Why must they grow up and lose it all?'"[7]

Mr. Ramsay: The Lighthouse – a stark tower of truth

Mrs. Ramsay dies, the house is left alone for years; she is a memory. Then the family returns, the children now teen-agers. Lily Briscoe is with them. The family is going to the Lighthouse. The day they go - Mr. Ramsay, his son James, and his daughter Cam - Lily stays behind. She finds in the house the old picture, takes up her abandoned work of art, and begins once again to paint. The children in the boat, now grown, observe their father, re-live their emotional battles with him, James re-envisioning the knife with which he wanted to stab him. He observes his father "getting his head now against the Lighthouse, now against the waste of waters running away into the open, like some old stone lying on the sand; he looked as if he had become physically what was always at the back of both of their minds – that loneliness which was for both of them the truth about things." [8]

Then they reach the Lighthouse: "So it was like that, James thought, the Lighthouse one had seen across the bay all these years; it was a stark tower on a bare rock. It satisfied him. It confirmed some obscure feeling of his about his own charac-ter."[9] Mr. Ramsay, who never praises James, says to him of his steering, "Well done!" At this moment of arrival, Lily finishes her picture: "With a sudden intensity, as if she saw it clear for a second she drew a line there in the centre. It was done; it was finished. Yes, she thought, laying down her brush in extreme fatigue, I have had my vision."[10] Only after Mrs. Ramsay is dead can this family go to the Lighthouse, can Mr. Ramsay begin to get beyond "Q," and can Lily finish her picture. They achieve the "big picture" conceived in their minds more than a decade earlier.

Confront the canvas the universe provides.

The family in *To the Lighthouse* is Virginia Woolf's family; the mother is her mother; the setting is their summer home. She adored her beautiful, albeit narcissistic mother; yet it was from her stern father, Leslie Stephen, that she took in the true grit required to be a writer. *To the Lighthouse* is Virginia Woolf's greatest literary achievement, and my brief summation here does not begin to do justice to her artistry as a writer. Our subject, however, is "the big picture," that is, the boundary that we all create around the vision for our life.

Every "big picture" is born into a climate of opinion. Many years ago I wrote a doctoral dissertation on Virginia Woolf's fiction and Post-Impressionist painting. As I look back upon my choice of subject matter, I realize that I related at a subconscious level with being pulled apart between two parents similar to the Ramsays, caught in their sentence upon my life. That moment of triumph, when Lily finishes her picture, symbolizes the necessity to leave behind the messages from the past and to confront the canvas the universe provides for us, to make our own mark upon life and upon our destiny. It requires a vision, and it requires the courage to set a navigation path to reach the Lighthouse.

How big can we think?

As Fuller observes, "If it is true that the bigger the thinking becomes the more lastingly effective it is, we must ask, 'How big can we think?' "[11] When Moses was led by the Lord up onto the mountain top, he was told that all the land he could envision, his feet could trod upon. It sounds simplistic to say that we can only be as big as we can think, but it is true. The circumference around our life is determined by our expectation, and our expectation is a reflection of our thought: the *Expectation*, the *Belief*, and the *Word*. "Expectation" is the first step to realization. If we can think it, if we can believe it, if we can speak it, then we can achieve it. Napoleon Hill tells us in *Think and Grow Rich*, "What the mind can conceive, it can achieve." Has anyone ever achieved more than his mind could conceive? Someone may tell us the good things that happened were "beyond my wildest dreams." Probably not!

Three big D's: Devotion, Dedication, Discipline

The dreams are wild because they are so "out there." We may even be afraid to have them in public, as Emily Dickinson says, "so public like a frog." When we make a public avowal, we make a spoken commitment. John F. Kennedy made a public avowal of a wild dream: putting a man on the moon. Once it was spoken, it became a possibility: *Expectation, Belief, Word.* He used the first industrial tool, the spoken word, to forge a commitment to a wild dream. When the "Big Picture" goes public, the forces marshal three big D's to make dreams reality: Devotion, Dedication, and Discipline. Without these, great ideas slip away into the residue of the little d's: down the drain of discarded dreams.

Corporate effort

Books have been written about the conception and achievement of the "big picture" of Henry Ford and Thomas Edison, of other great thinkers and doers. I have chosen here to bring this down to a homely level, to a story in which I have personal involvement. We often feel intimidated because it seems as if one man does it alone. The truth is Henry Ford's "big picture" could not be realized without the efforts of the Ford Motor Company; John Kennedy's "big picture" could not be realized without NASA.

Down to earth

The life story, the lifeline, in my father's family effectively illustrates the necessity that the "big picture" be publicly declared and collectively adopted for it to be realized and achieved. The word must be spoken to mobilize the resources. Then the individual's commitment to the three big D's: Devotion, Dedication and Discipline have a medium in which to unfold, even when the prevailing climate of opinion, filled with doubts and hesitation, fails to nurture and support the "big picture." I have chosen this story as an illustration because it is closer to home for most of us who do not foresee becoming a Ford or an Edison, a Bill Gates or a Steve Jobs, a Mark Zuckerberg or a Sheryl Sandberg.

Two "homely" examples

A big picture gone awry

My father was in the middle of twelve children born to a wiry and intelligent Ohio farmer and a woman from an Illinois family whose members were notable for their large, tall frames, and a set of the jaw known as "Jim jaw." This was a common designation where I come from. I'm not sure exactly who "Jim" was originally, but I know that all of my great aunts and great uncles on my grandmother's side had it. It is a set of the jaw, slightly protruding, firm, unmoving, symbolic of steadfast determination. If the determination were in your favor, you would be flushed with confidence. If the determination were against you, you felt like a whipped dog, actually victimized by the set of the jaw of the one who is an antagonist to any project or idea, especially yours.

Dead set Jim jaw

My grandmother's "Jim jaw" was dead set against my grandfather. He gave up his farm in Ohio, moved to southern Michigan, and bought a coal yard. As the story goes, he put the coal yard on the line for a section of land in the Upper Peninsula of Michigan. A section, you will recall, is big, 640 acres. The Upper Peninsula is rugged, with a long, dark winter, a short summer and growing season, still, even today, relatively desolate, predominately wooded timber and iron country. The Detroit automakers used to take their enemies up to the corporate "hideaway" for deer hunting and bump them off, by accident, the first day of deer season. Perhaps they still do. Who would know the difference?

The people who settled in this remote place came from Sweden and Norway. It reminded them of home. Since I spent twenty-five years with my former husband's family driving back and forth to a cabin in the Upper Peninsula, 500 miles each way, to a spot on a lake that for many of those years had only a rude cabin with a pump and an outhouse, I can appreciate my grandmother's point of view. She was a sitter, not a doer; a bystander, not an innovator; a user of goods, not a maker; a receiver, not an initiator. There is a saying in the Midwest, "Aunt Mame sits broad." My grandmother's name was Flora May, and she sat broad. I loved her to pieces as my grandmother with the welcome lap. She was a Mrs. Ramsay. Had I been my grandfather, I wouldn't have chosen her as my "helpmate."

Desperate: out of hope

My grandfather's name was Edward Wood, and I suspect a part of him felt chained to "dead wood" when it came to his dreams and his vision. He wanted to relocate and start a new life. That was his "big picture." My grandmother refused to go. The idea of cultivating that 640 acres of forest and farm land was my grandfather's "big picture," but my grandmother did not buy into it. The lips closed firmly, the jaw went "Jim," and the issue was deadened in hostile silence.

My grandfather deserted. He just flat ran away and left my grandmother with that whole houseful of kids, ten of them. Twice he returned, and twice my grandmother was pregnant again. All my childhood I was told my grandfather was a despicable man, today's dead beat dad. In retrospect, I wonder whether the desertion was an act of desperation. That's what the word *desperate* means: out of hope.

Dismal Great Depression

Whatever my grandfather's feelings may have been about the destruction of his dreams, he was irresponsible to his wife and his children and wreaked great hardship upon them. During those depression years, there was scarcely enough to eat; and they survived by the charity of Mr. Cohn who owned the corner grocery store and "ran a bill" for the family. Grandma made milk gravy; the children took turns eating meat. The oldest son, Chester, worked at the cigar store and brought his entire pay every week home to his mother to care for the family. It was said he had a girlfriend, but we never met her; and his life was placed on hold for his mother and brothers and sisters. He died at forty, before he ever had a chance to have a life of his own. Since I stayed with my grandmother during the day while my parents worked, I remember running to meet Uncle Chester every Friday afternoon when he got his paycheck. He always stopped at Mr. Cohn's to get me a vanilla ice cream cone. That's when vanilla was pure, the ice cream was made with real cream, and nothing ever tasted so good.

A big picture realized.

One might say the dashing of my grandfather's "big picture" created the climate of opinion in which my father's "big picture" could be sparked and ignited. All of the twelve children worked; and my father, from the age of ten, was a caddy at the Lenawee County Golf Club. During the summer he would spend the nights there, sleeping outside, because it was too far to ride his bicycle home. He developed an early love of golf which he retained until his death. The men who hired him as their caddy were the wealthiest citizens in the county, and he also came to hold the vision of himself with a large wad of bills in his pocket, readily able to pay for anything.

His name was LeRoy, in French meaning "the king: *Le Roi.* He was a Leo. Since he was very bright, he skipped grades in school, and graduated at 15. He always regretted that, because he felt he wasn't mature enough to make good decisions. He took a job at the Simplex Paper Corporation in Adrian, Michigan at the age of 15, and entered a life as a factory worker, first doing drafting, then eventually being promoted into management, overseeing the shipping: traffic manager. He married my mother when he was 22 and she was 21.

The factory: chained

The factory was the life source for my father's family. My uncles all worked in a factory or foundry. I think it is fair to say that my father was the most intelligent male in the family, only matched by my Aunt Cora who, were she born later, would have run a town or a company or even a country the way she ran her twelve siblings and her church. The Simplex Paper Corporation, the factory where my father worked, in my mother's mind became the place where my father would be chained and rot; his staying there to her symbolized lack of initiative and drive. When they fought, and they fought frequently and violently, all my childhood, she would say to him, "You're just yellow, and you'll never get out of that Simplex." My father's early childhood experiences made security very important for him, and he was fearful to let go of stability, his piano top.

The union and the corporation

The company, the Simplex, noted in my father the same thing my mother did, the inner resources and ability to be more and do more. My father displayed his leadership ability quickly, and when he was in his late 20s, held an executive position in the Michigan CIO labor union. It was soon after a big convention in Grand Rapids, Michigan where my father was elected to an office, that the company promoted him. They probably feared his power as a potential troublemaker and moved him into management to get him out of the union. I was only five years old at the time and do not recall the conversations about the promotion, but I suspect that he was lured by the increase in money and the control over his time. For whatever reason, the navigation path he chose then was crucial, because it opened a new horizon for his thinking.

The entrepreneural spirit

My parents were entrepreneurs in their hearts, but neither was capable without the other. My father had the mind, the thought, the plan. He was a high **C** with almost equal high **D**. My mother, a high **I**, had communication and a power of execution. As a farm girl, she didn't mind hard work, long hours, doing whatever it took to get a job done, even the most menial of **S**-type tasks. Together they were a synergetic union. Once my father was in management, he could take phone calls at work and come and go more freely. He and my mother accepted an invitation from my Uncle Bill and Aunt Connie, who had a successful clothing business in nearby Blissfield, to go into a clothing business with them.

Mother left the factory to work full-time in the store. It was a glorious place for her. She expressed her flair for fashion by buying for the store. She was always at least two years ahead in her ability to pick styles and colors. Her great people personality emerged in her interaction with the customers, and she brought warmth and sparkle to the endeavor. My father, who was meticulous in everything he did, discovered a talent for measuring men for tailored suits, and soon they had a flourishing business. Uncle Bill and Aunt Connie seldom came in the store.

The vision

Some personal life changes, apparent reversals, again moved my father closer to his "big picture." My mother became pregnant after several miscarriages, and the doctor told her she would have to have complete rest to carry this baby to full term. My parents sold out their half of the store. Without them, the store went under; and my aunt and uncle never spoke to any of us again. As a store owner, however, my father had become active in the Jr. Chamber of Commerce; and given his natural leadership ability, he was elected president. One of the projects of the JC's was to draft a plan for a municipal golf course. With his love of golf, he had worked on the project and was an ardent advocate. The City, however, turned down the idea as too costly for such a small community, at that time around 18,000 people. One summer, when I was fifteen, my father took my mother out for her first game of golf. She had a wonderful time; and when he told her that he had always dreamed of building a golf course, she said, "Let's do it."

The execution

My father had the idea and the executive decision-making; my mother had the personality to attract a clientele and the willingness to do whatever it took to get the job done, whether that meant mowing fairways or cleaning the pro-shop. Unlike my father's parents before him, my parents had the right combination to succeed, together. They had the three D's to realize their big picture: Devotion, Dedication and Discipline. Public avowal, however, was painful. My parents bought a 65-acre cow pasture and began to build this "golf course."

It's very much like a *Field of Dreams*: build a place and they will come. The first year my grandfather came and planted a crop of rye to give the grass a foundation. Since all of my parents' saved resources went into the purchase of the land, the process of building this golf course was totally hands-on. My father continued his job at the Simplex and came after a full day's work to work for himself. The greens were hand built with a shovel and a rake. We planted the Seaside Bent grass seed; and as the seedlings began to sprout, my mother and I weeded the grass on our hands and knees. My father laid out the course. The first three years you couldn't tell the rough from the fairway. It was all rough.

The navigation path

In the middle of this enterprise, my father became ill. When he went into the hospital, he weighed 220 pounds; he emerged from the hospital at 135. He was essentially an invalid, unable to work at his job or to help with the golf course. This left my mother and me. Out of financial necessity, we opened the golf course a year too early. It was, indeed, a rough play. The barn on the property became our pro shop, right where the cow stalls had been. Later we even sold the house in town and moved into the upstairs of that barn. At first we had no rest rooms, only a chemical toilet upstairs in the loft where the hay had been kept. We had no sprinkler system. I would get up a 4:00 a.m. and begin my day watering greens.

The reasons for complaint were manifold. Also, initiative evokes envy. Local people were so resentful of my parents' steadfastness to their dream that many refused to come out and play on the course. Even our relatives jeered at us. Our clientele came mostly over the border from Ohio, and we were bitterly assaulted with criticism from the first players because the course was not ready. This is where the "Devotion, Dedication, and Discipline" became so essential. We stuck to it. Work was all we knew.

A realization at great cost

The course improved. Local golf leagues began to play. My father got better. He began to collect the money from cart rentals as a roll of $1 bills to be used for tree money. Until his death, he had that roll of bills in his pocket, his adolescent image of prosperity. My parents planted trees. They acquired more land, an adjacent orchard. They built another nine holes. When they finally sold the golf course to retire to Florida, it was one of the finest eighteen-hole public courses in southern Michigan. They had realized their big picture.

The "Big Picture" reboot

Expectation, Belief, and *Word* in action

What are the lessons we can draw from this? *Expectation, Belief,* and *Word*:

1) The mental "big picture," *Expectation*, is essential to successful creation.

2) Collective adoption of the "big picture," *Belief*, marshals the resources to bring the "wild dream" into reality.

3) Public avowal, the *Word*, is an important part of the commitment process. When you speak your *Word*, you

bring the idea into focus; you plant the seed and express your intent to nurture it and to make it grow.

4) The 3 D's, Devotion, Dedication, and Discipline, make it happen.

5) The big picture must be broken down into manageable, reachable, measurable goals.

6) A navigation path must be set, each goal reached becoming a stepping-stone to the next.

Chunked down and accomplished

Note within this process that each step was an individual goal to be chunked down and then accomplished: The acquisition of the land, the rye grass base, the lay out of the course, the assembly of the basic tools and machinery, the building of the greens and the tees, the transformation of a cow barn into a pro shop, the stocking of the retail store. Each step had to be achieved to put it all together. Note each element has within it a measurable goal, a point at which achievement can be determined. Had I known then what I know now about real estate, we would have added another step and built houses around the periphery, becoming one of the first golf course developers.

Navigation: dismissing macrocosmic and microcosmic irrelevancies

The best thing about a navigation path is that it can be changed. Storms do come up unexpectedly. My parents never expected my father's prolonged illness. You can go at the same goal with the same big picture in mind from a different direction or with a different timetable. When you have a navigation path, you are the captain of your ship, you are the maker of your fate. You can reboot over and over again.

Remember, only energy and thought exist. Just as you can control your navigation path, you can control your thinking. As Fuller tells us, "Thinking itself consists of self-disciplined dismissal of both the macrocosmic and microcosmic irrelevancies which leaves only the lucidly-relevant considerations."[13] When you conceive your big picture, consider fear of failure and fear of inadequacy as "irrelevancies." Any previous limits you have set for yourself are "irrelevancies."

Babylon is an outstanding example of man's ability to achieve great objectives, using whatever means are at his disposal. All of the resources supporting this large city were man-developed. All of it riches were man-made.

George, S. Clason, The Richest Man in Babylon [1]

Wealth has its source in applications of the mind to nature, from the rudest strokes of spade and axe up to the last secrets of art. Intimate ties subsist between thought and all production; because a better order is equivalent to vast amounts of brute labor.

Emerson, "Wealth" [2]

All is waste and worthless, till
Arrives the wise selecting will,
And, out of slime and chaos, Wit
Draws the threads of fair and fit.
Then temples rose, and towns, and marts,
The shop of toil, the hall of arts.

Emerson, Wealth [3]

TRUE WEALTH

Not one iota of yesterday

SHALL WE SAY necessity is the mother of rebooting? Since we cannot change one iota of yesterday, yesterday's disaster either motivates us to start over or we go under. It is essential to know we have the resources beyond material goods by which we normally measure "wealth." If we set our navigation path in accordance with our "big picture" and our ship sinks, what happens? To illustrate this point, Fuller describes a billionaire in a shipwreck:

> Now I'm going to have a man in a shipwreck. He's rated as a very rich man, worth over a billion dollars by all of society's accredited conceptions of real wealth. He has taken with him on his voyage all his stocks and bonds, all his property deeds, all his checkbooks, and, to play it safe, has brought along a lot of diamonds and gold bullion. The ship burns and sinks, and there are no lifeboats, for they, too, have burned. If our billionaire holds on to his gold, he's going to sink a little faster than the others. So I would say he hadn't much left either of now or tomorrow in which

to articulate his wealth, and since wealth cannot work backwardly his kind of wealth is vitally powerless. It is really a worthless pile of chips of an arbitrary game which we are playing and does not correspond to the accounting processes of our real universe's evolutionary transactions. Obviously the catastrophied billionaire's kind of wealth has no control over either yesterday, now, or tomorrow. He can't extend his life with that kind of wealth unless he can persuade the one passenger who has a life-jacket to yield that only means of extending one life in exchange for one crazy moment's sense of possession of all the billion-aire's sovereign-powers-backed legal tender, all of which the catastrophy-disillusioned and only moments ear-lier "powerfully rich" and now desperately helpless man would thankfully trade for the physical means of extend-ing the years of his life; or of his wife.[4]

Not measured in goods

So now what? If wealth is not derived from pieces of paper, hunks of metal, stones, sovereignty-acquired interests in land, or theoretical ownership of enterprises, is not measured in gold, diamonds, currency, real estate deeds of trusts, stocks and bonds, then what is it? These can all be taken away. How many times have you been shipwrecked? When that happens, what is left? Fuller defines true wealth as "our ability to deal successfully with our forward energetic regeneration," or in other words, our ability to reboot.

Wealth as metaphysical know-how can only increase.

He breaks it down into two parts, physical energy and metaphysical know-how, observing that we cannot run out of either one. Einstein's formula, $E=MC^2$ proves that energy as matter and energy as radiation are interchangeable variants, and building upon this "know-how, physicists have determined that physical energy is conserved, cannot be exhausted: Energy is finite and infinitely conserved."[6] Wealth, defined as metaphysical know-how, can only increase. We cannot learn less. Every time we make an experiment, we can only learn more. Every time we solve a problem, our wealth increases. Forget yesterday. It is over. Wealth by this standard is our mental, physical, spiritual ability to cope with the present and to plan and mold the future. The more we use it, the wealthier we are.

True wealth: *The Edge*

If you have never seen the film *The Edge* with Anthony Hopkins and Alec Baldwin, I suggest you do. *The Edge* features a billionaire, played by Anthony Hopkins, married to an incredibly beautiful model, who is having an affair with Alec Baldwin, a photographer. Hopkins has accompanied his wife, the photographer, and the camera crew on a photo shoot. As the movie begins, they prepare to take off in Hopkins' personal plane over snow-capped peaks and icy-gray water to a remote lodge.

Lost in the Wilds

Hopkins, who has an encyclopedic memory, has been reading a book, *Lost in the Wilds*, a birthday gift given to him by his secretary before he left on the trip. Although Hopkins considers this gift a curious choice, it becomes quickly apparent that Baldwin and Hopkins' wife are having an affair; and one comes to suspect from the start that Baldwin, and perhaps Baldwin and the wife together, have a plot to kill the billionaire husband on this trip. The secretary may have anticipated this. As they board the plane, Hopkins' assistant tells him the weather should be agreeable and they should have no problems so long as they avoid flying at a height where they might encounter migrating geese. They plan to be gone just overnight, returning the next evening.

The rabbit and the panther

The book, *Lost in the Wild*, is just one of several highly symbolic items introduced at the opening of the film. Baldwin gives Hopkins a knife, and the lodge keeper says Hopkins must give him a coin, lest the cord of friendship be cut. The wife gives Hopkins a watch, affectionately engraved, "To the only man I have ever loved." He is moved. Baldwin is also wearing a new watch. We learn later that Baldwin's watch, a gift from the same woman, bears an engraving thanking him for "all the nights." Hopkins, whose conversation is learned and clever, is an endless storehouse of knowledge, facts, and information. It flows from him spontaneously. The lodge keeper, thinking he can trip him up, offers Hopkins $5 to tell him what is on the back of a wooden paddle with a panther on the front. Hopkins says, "It's a rabbit taking a rest." The lodge keeper turns over the paddle, and behold, Hopkins is right. The lodge keeper asks why the rabbit is taking a rest, and Hopkins replies, "Because the rabbit is smarter than the panther." Baldwin is the panther, Hopkins the rabbit.

The migrating geese

Circumstances cause Baldwin to go in search of a local trapper for a photo shoot. Hopkins, goaded on by his wife, accompanies him and one of his crew. They find a note on the trapper's cabin door that he is hunting at a spot about twenty miles north of his cabin, and they proceed to that site. During the plane ride, with his ironic humor, Baldwin picks at Hopkins about the isolation, aloofness, separation of a rich man who can never know whether people really like him or whether they want something from them. Hopkins always replies, "Never feel sorry for a man who owns a plane." He asks Baldwin what he wants from him. Baldwin says he likes his wife. Just as Hopkins asks, "How are you planning to kill me?" the plane, flying low, collides with a flock of migrating geese. The geese break through the windshield, the plane goes down, and Hopkins, Baldwin, and Baldwin's assistant are the only survivors. They are lost in the frigid wild. Because Baldwin brought with him the note on the trapper's door, no one knows their destination.

Never feel sorry for a man who owns a plane

This man who owns a plane is by far the strongest of the three, not only in brainpower, but also in perseverance and courage. Hopkins emerges as the master mind, the problem solver, the center of their survival. He has with him literally only the clothes on his back, the knife Baldwin has just given him as a birthday present, the knowledge lodged in his brain, and an indomitable spirit. The survival book, which Hopkins was reading, is lost when they sink. The plot of the story pits man against man, man against himself, and man against bear, a Kodiak bear, about which they were warned by the lodge keeper, "Once this bear has tasted human flesh, it craves it."

The Kodiak bear

Hopkins draws upon every bit of knowledge he has. To set a course toward the south, he makes a magnet from a needle. A Kodiak bear finds them and begins to pursue them. They escape by toppling a log over the top of a waterfall. Hopkins is the last one over the log, precariously keeping his balance as the bear aggressively jumps up and down on the end. Hopkins falls into the river, and the other two scramble and stretch to save him from going over the waterfall. Baldwin tells Hopkins he was saved because they couldn't afford to lose him. This leaves Hopkins strangely moved. Baldwin jests that Hopkins probably never had a friend. Hopkins reminds him, "Never feel sorry for a man who owns a plane."

Shame

When they discover this arduous adventure only leads them back to where they began, a walk in a circle, Baldwin and the assistant become hysterical. Hopkins admonishes them, "Why do men die in the woods. They die of shame." Hopkins surmises his magnet didn't work because of his metal belt buckle. While he re-thinks their course, he attempts to distract the assistant from his fear by asking him to carve a spear from a stick with his knife. The assistant injures himself, a deep wound, and his blood draws the bear who attacks and devours him, leaving now only Hopkins and Baldwin and the bear who has tasted human flesh. When the stalking, flesh-craving bear becomes too much of a threat, Hopkins decides they must be the aggressor; they must kill the bear. He incites Baldwin to action by yelling, "Kill the Bear!" and the cry, "What one man can do, another can do." They lure the bear to fall on a spear, his weight becoming the force that kills him, a skillful implementation of leverage.

For all the nights: the dead fall

When Hopkins and Baldwin finally reach an abandoned cabin, it is near a river and houses a canoe. Baldwin, who can now see his way out on his own, is ready to carry out his original intent, to kill Hopkins. Hopkins, taking the warranty out of the watch box as paper to start a fire, finds the engravings ordered for the two watches by his wife. For the third time in the film, he asks to see Baldwin's watch. For the third time, Baldwin tells him the watch is broken. When Hopkins quotes the engraving, "for all the nights," Baldwin knows that Hopkins knows. He points the gun he found in the cabin at Hopkins; but Hopkins, unafraid, knowing Baldwin is a coward at heart, lures him, as he earlier lured the bear, to step on a bear trap, a dead fall. Baldwin falls into the hole and is impaled on the waiting spear. Even though Hopkins makes every effort to treat his wound and to take him out by canoe, Baldwin dies just as the search helicopter catches sight of them on the ground and comes in to rescue. Baldwin does a last good deed, saying "It's never too late for a kind gesture," by telling Hopkins his wife knew nothing of the murder plan.

Something unequivocal

Hopkins is the only survivor. He, too, makes a "kind gesture" by telling the press that the two dead men died saving his life. He, the rabbit, outsmarts both the bear and the panther. Hopkins' survival demonstrates his true wealth in action, the problem solving ability that empowered him not only to deal with his present circumstances but also to plan and forge ahead for his future, his regenerative power. He tells Baldwin, "All my life I wanted to do something unequivocal." The man who comes out of the wild is a far richer man than the one who went into the wild, for his wealth was tested and found adequate. He proved his capacity to cope with the present and to move purposefully and energetically toward the forward days of his life. His know-how expanded. We cannot learn less.

Symbolic and emblematic

Four statements from this film become symbolic, emblematic:

1) Never feel sorry for a man who owns a plane.

2) Why do men die in the woods? They die of shame.

3) Kill the bear!

4) What one man can do, another can do!

Not the root of all evil.

When Hopkins comments, "Never feel sorry for a man who owns a plane," he is expressing a counter to the race conscious-ness - climate of opinion idea we carry around: If one is rich monetarily, one must be miserable. The statement "money is the root of all evil" is used to justify not having any; when in fact, the statement rendered correctly is "*love of* money is the root of all evil," covetousness.

Actually, the free flow of funds, prosperity, a constant cir-culation of money in and out of a household, whether symbol-ized by a roll of bills in the pocket or a wad of bills on a money clip, eliminates at least half of the reason a marriage and family fall apart, financial stress: making ends meets, spouses accus-ing each other of not bringing in enough, spouses too strung out from struggle to have time or energy to be intimate with each other, fathers running away when they can't take it, turn-ing to alcohol or drugs. Hopkins is "complete;" Baldwin is not. If you have an issue with people who have money, get over it. When Donald Trump was interrogated about his bankruptcies, he replied, "I will always be rich." It is a mind-set. Have you told yourself, "I will always be poor?" Expectation, Belief, Word. **Time to reboot: Change your thinking, change your speaking, change your life.**

Fear of not being enough

Hopkins observes, "Why do men die in the woods? They die of shame." This takes us back to "no mistakes." Survival in the woods tests physical endurance and mental alacrity, steadfastness of purpose and cunning. One feels completely exposed, naked. As Emily Dickinson says, "somebody" is "naked like a frog." Shame comes from fear of not being "enough" and doing it in public, whether observed by a human being, a bear, or a squirrel. When King Lear in Shakespeare's play makes a rash decision to accept his evil daughters' flattery and to abandon his faithful one, Cordelia, he also banishes his faithful servant, Kent. Kent, foreseeing Lear's mistreatment by his evil daughters, comes to Lear in disguise and asks to serve him. Lear, naked in the storm, exposed to the elements, gone mad because of the betrayal of his daughters and the loss of his retinue of soldiers, reduced from grandeur to homelessness, speaks to Kent:

> What wouldst thou?
> Service.
> Who wouldst thou serve?
> You.
> Dost thou know me, fellow?
> No, sire; but you have that in your countenance which I would fain call "master."

What's that?
Authority.

King Lear, Act I, sc. iv, ll .24-31

Men die of shame in the woods because they have lost touch with their inner "authority," with their identity, with their center. Peter Goldberg, a psychoanalytic historian at UCLA, researched the reasons why the victims of the holocaust, learned, capable, intelligent professional human beings, allowed themselves to be herded and slaughtered like cattle. He concluded that when their clothes were removed, when they were naked, they no longer had the outer reinforcing symbolic garments to remind them of their identity as effective human beings. They lost their "authority"; they died of shame. "Why do men die in the woods? They die of shame.

The cry of the hunter: Kill the Bear!

To "Kill the Bear!" Hopkins and Baldwin need to call upon every atom of adrenalin their bodies can produce. This cry, "Kill the Bear!" organizes the human body and spirit in purpose, in cause, in determination, in defiance against weakness and vulnerability. At this moment, every other concern in life falls away. It is a commitment one makes to life, to continue living; and the human body and spirit rise to the occasion. When Hopkins accompanies "Kill the Bear!" with "What one man can do, another can do!" he is bringing Baldwin, the weaker of the two, along with him. These words penetrate his mind and spirit, and his inner resources marshal to the occasion.

To the edge of possibility

We do not know who we are until we are tested. This is true leadership. When Emerson describes Napoleon leading his men up, into, and across the mountains, he did it with the battle cry, "There shall be no Alps." And there were no Alps. The Alps were conquered. Napoleon, says Emerson, "Went to the edge of his possibility." [8] The same thing happens to Baldwin as he is challenged by Hopkins: "What one man can do another can do!" Hopkins and Baldwin act with a most remarkable synergy to perform a super-human feat. Battle cries have been used throughout the ages by primitive tribes preparing for the hunt, by soldiers preparing to meet the enemy: "What one man can do, another can do!" "Kill the Bear!" Hopkins all his life has wanted to do "something unequivocal." When he goes to the "edge of his possibility," when he kills the bear, it is done.

The "Store of Knowledge": Moore's Law

The metaphysical know-how demonstrated by Hopkins in the film cannot be purchased. Every time we use it, we have more, because we cannot learn less. This is true wealth, i.e. the stored data with the know-how to use it. In 1965 Gordon Moore predicted the capacity of a computer chip would double every year. When that proved out, in 1975 he predicted the chip capacity would double every two years. In 1995 it was doubling every eighteen months. This average rate of increase, doubling every eighteen months, is now called "Moore's Law." That means our access to data or to information is doubling at that speed. That is why Silicon Valley, which prospers by intellectual property, is filled with stories of success.

Exponential Function

This doubling of numbers is the "exponential function." It is illustrated in the fable of the Indian king who asked the man who invented the game of chess what reward he would like. The inventor used the sixty-four chessboard squares as a basis for his request. He asked that one grain of wheat be placed on the first square, and that on each successive square, the amount be doubled that of the previous one. By square eight he had 255; by square sixteen 65,535; by square twenty-four 8.4 million. [10] Think about doing this with a single penny. The popular program "Who Wants to be a Millionaire?" effectively demonstrated the exponential function. In just sixteen questions, the contestants who continue to win can move up to $1,000,000 by doubling the wager on each question. The unlimited growth and application of knowledge, of know-how, is true wealth in action. It walks around with us, in us, available to us at every living moment. The more we use it, the more we have.

Immigration: True Wealth in action

We are facing a refugee crisis on the planet with the millions who have fled the civil war in Syria and the political unrest throughout the Middle East and parts of Africa.

Those who have fled liquidated their material resources to secure passage, often from pirates. These people carry with them only their "true wealth," their problem solving know-how. A similar population emigrated to the U.S. in the mid-seventies after the fall of Saigon in 1975. They were granted special immigration opportunities because they had been vigorously engaged in our American effort in the Viet Nam War and had worked intimately with our personnel. In their past lives many of these immigrants were business-men, doctors, pharmacists, generals, mayors, leaders, professional people with high degrees and training. When the North Vietnamese Communists took over, the homes and possessions of the men and their families were seized, the men were placed in "Re-education camps," concentration camps, and the women and the children were left to fend for themselves, without resources.

Women in new roles

The women, for the most part, had been in traditional family roles, with husbands to provide for them and the family. They found themselves now head of the households, forced to work, to scratch to earn a living for the first time, with everything against them because they were rejected, outside the Communist establishment. These women, especially, discovered within themselves resilience and an ability to meet challenges for growth that would have remained undiscovered. They re-booted. An ability to do needlework turned them into seamstresses; an ability to cook turned them into vendors of their best dishes at the market; an ability to argue and bargain turned them into merchants, buying and selling, trading to keep alive. The wives not only had to take care of the family left at home, but also they needed to visit their husbands in the Re-Education Camps to augment the meager rations provided by the Communists. Often this required a long trip, ten to twelve hours in a single day, or sometimes several days, of travel. The women worked collectively to support one another.

Boat people

When the men returned home, there was nothing of their former life to be recaptured. They collectively conceived of a "big picture" of coming to the United States to create a new life for themselves. They were able to mobilize the three big D's: devotion, dedication, and discipline. To pay for the travel, they sold whatever material wealth they still possessed: gold, jewels, art. The Vietnamese have stories of the harrowing voyages that they undertook, attacked by pirates, robbed, raped, and pillaged.

Holding camps

Those who were successful in their voyages found themselves in holding camps in Malaysia, in Singapore, in the Philippines, waiting until a sponsor would assist them to come here to the United States. When they finally arrived here, they were without funds, without the language, without a job, often without even a relative to care for them. They didn't know how to drive a car, even how to operate the household appliances we all take for granted. Yet, they went to work. They got jobs at minimum wage. They went to school at night to learn English as a second language. They worked together. They lived together, saved money, purchased property.

Little Saigon

In the area of Orange County in California, designated Little Saigon, you can chart by street the movement of this hard-working, self-disciplined, intelligent, persevering group of immigrants. As their neighborhood expands, they improve the environment. The streets are neat and tidy; their shops, stores, and professional offices have clean windows; their homes and apartment buildings are in good repair with flowers planted in the yards. Purposeful activity directs their movement. Education is held in the highest place in this community, only second to the family. If we wonder why UCLA is an anagram for "United Caucasians Lost among Asians," and why the University of California at Irvine is dominated by Asians, it is because the Asian immigrants have a" big picture" with definite goals, work hard, never quit, and tirelessly seek to use and develop every bit of God-given *true wealth* that they have.

Lofty aspirations

Their aspirations, their big pictures are lofty. They want to be medical doctors, dentists, pharmacists, engineers, computer network specialists, computer programmers, accountants, financial analysts, teachers, nurses. They are making a great contribution to our culture by sharing the intensity of their commitment to excellence. A friend who has been a patient at the VA Hospital speaks of the improved care since Vietnamese medical residents are on the staff.

Elementary school teachers who have Vietnamese students tell me that they are their best students. It was exemplified for me one day when I was having my nails done at, yes, a Vietnamese nail salon. The daughter of the owner, seven years old, answers the phone, makes the change, and places the orders for her mother. Very pleased with herself and extremely self-confident, she told me that she knew three languages: Vietnamese, English, and Mexican. I said, "Well, 'Mexican' is actually 'Spanish.'" "Oh," she said, elated, "Then I know four languages: Vietnamese, English, Mexican, and Spanish."

Risk-taking visionaries: our national wealth

Most of us came at one time from the same risk-taking, visionary, persevering, self-disciplined stock as this immigrant group. This is the "true wealth" of the American Society. We have been able to convert the capital wealth of this country to greater productivity and expansion by the constant increase of our metaphysical know-how. When we regard wealth in this way, there can only be expansion, exponential expansion. This means there can only be increased abundance, that there is enough. The official U.S. Census of 1810 valued the national wealth of the United States at three billion dollars. At that time we had no telegraph, no electro-magnetics, no mass-produced steel, no railroads, no wireless, no X-ray, no electric light, no power by wire, no electric motor, no knowledge of atoms or electrons, no computers, no internet. All of these discoveries and a myriad more have been made through the exercise of our true wealth, our metaphysical know how.

Metaphysical and monetary wealth: interconnected

Notice how integrally connected are metaphysical wealth and monetary wealth with intellectual property-based enterprises: software, Internet, communication, social media, automation. Should we, as "ordinary" citizens, feel incapacitated when we don't understand how everything works? Each day new tools are created for us to use to reboot. Jack Ma, the creator of Alibaba, the world largest internet retailer, admits he doesn't understand how the internet works.

Look around you and find a problem you can solve. AIRBNB was born when Brian Chesky and his roommate moved to San Francisco after graduating from the Rhode Island School of Design. There was a Design Convention, and they were broke. He had the idea to make a little extra money by offering space on his floor on air mattresses. That was the beginning of AIRBNB.

That's only one element of the "Share Economy." With Uber and Lyft we have ride sharing and job sharing. So many people are out of work. What can you create to serve a need that will give someone a job. There's a buzz about the IKEA factor, approaching problems with something that sells us on ourselves because we do it ourselves. The new Fresh Meal embraces the IKEA factor. A box containing fresh ingredients and a recipe is delivered to your door so you can make your own meal.

True wealth only grows. Nothing truly exists except the mind in action as thought. As we take control of our thinking and tap into our true wealth, our wealth multiplies exponentially.

PART 5: REPLANT

* **LEVERAGE**

* **SYNERGY**

* **GREAT PIRATE**

In our society there is a standing antagonism between the conservative and the democratic classes; between those who have made their fortunes, and the young and the poor who have fortunes to make; between the interests of dead labor – that is, the labor of hands long ago still in the grave, which labor is now entombed in money stocks, or in land and buildings owned by idle capitalists – and the interests of living labor, which seeks to possess itself of land and buildings and money stocks.

Emerson, "Napoleon; or, The Man of the World" [1]

LEVERAGE

MORE WITH LESS

The ancient practice of usury

IT USED TO be the practice in public schools for children to be required to memorize this passage from one of Shakespeare's best-known plays, *The Merchant of Venice*:

> The quality of mercy is not strained,
> It droppeth as the gentle rain from heaven
> Upon the place beneath. It is twice blest;
> It blesseth him that gives and him that takes.
> 'Tis mightiest in the mightiest. It becomes
> The throned monarch better than his crown.
> His scepter shows the force of temporal power,
> The attribute to awe and majesty
> Wherein doth sit the dread and fear of kings.
> But mercy is above this sceptered sway
> It is enthroned in the heart of kings,
> It is an attribute to God himself,

And earthly power doth then show likest God's
When mercy seasons justice.

Act IV, Sc. 1, ll. 184-197

This speech is made as a plea to the Jew, Shylock, who has accepted a pound of flesh as the interest due from a Christian for borrowed money. In ancient times this practice was called *usury*, because the interest charged is for the *use* of the money. Christians spurned this Jewish practice, considered it wrong. In the play, the borrower, Antonio, a Christian and a great pirate, loses his argosy from Tripoli at sea. His creditors swoop in on him, and he is declared bankrupt. This is Shylock's moment; he will have his revenge, his pound of flesh. A trial is called. Portia, in this famous speech, asks Shylock to show mercy. When Shylock refuses mercy, the tide turns against him. He may take the pound of flesh, "but not one drop of blood." Further, he, an alien, has sought to take the life of a citizen. For this he, Shylock, can die. The Duke resolves it by a pardon for Shylock's life, but grants Antonio half of all that Shylock possesses.

Interest: our usury-driven economy

Such a bitter confrontation over the charging of interest seems almost unfathomable today, *so usury*-driven is our economy. In fact, we have just emerged from the sub-prime mortgage debacle that caused hundreds of thousands of families to lose their homes and the U.S government to step in to save the banks because they were "too big to fail." This caused the worst Recession since the Great Depression and put many people out of work. The interest rates plummeted in order to help get the economy back on track.

This follows Keynesian Economics, a policy the United States adopted at the end of the Great Depression. It is based on the ideas the British economist, Maynard Keynes, published in 1936 in *The General Theory of Employment, Interest and Money*. When the unemployment rate goes down, the interest rate goes up. When the unemployment rate goes up, the interest rate goes down. The psychology of the marketplace is this: If more people are working and earning and spending, the economy risks inflation. To "cool" inflation worries, we must pay at the bank. The role of the Head of the Federal Reserve assumes great power because the one in that role determines how much money will be available for ordinary citizens to use. The rate of interest charged for the use of money either curtails or accelerates our spending practice.

Maynard Keynes reasoned that a man with money, like Shylock, has a choice. He can choose to lend his money for interest, or he can keep it liquid.

> ...we can usefully employ the ancient distinction between the use of money for the transaction of current business and its use as a store of wealth. As regards the first of these two uses, it is obvious that up to a point it is worthwhile to sacrifice a certain amount of interest for the convenience of liquidity. But, given that the rate of interest is never negative, why should anyone prefer to hold his wealth in a form which yields little or no interest to holding it in a form which yields interest. . ? [2]

Keynes continues with the choice between lending money for interest or investing it in capital assets:

> The owner of wealth, who has been induced not to hold his wealth in the shape of hoarded money, still has two alternatives between which to choose. He can lend his money at the current rate of money-interest or he can purchase some kind of capital asset.[3]

If the wealthy man buys stocks, a capital asset, and the stock market is inflated, that is, the earnings of the company do not warrant the price of the stock, then the wealthy man may think he is wealthier than he is and take risks. He may borrow on margin to buy more, and thus drive up the price of the stock higher.

Interest and leverage

Ordinary citizens consider themselves fortunate if they can acquire a home as their capital asset. When they borrow money and pay interest for the use of the money, they are using *leverage*. The abundance of capital assets and the success of our economy has been the result of effective use of leverage. Many of the wonderful things in our life that we take for granted, the factories that produce goods, the banks that circulate money and help us buy houses and start businesses, the schools and parks and concert halls and theaters, got here by leverage. The Christian distaste for the idea of paying interest, expressed by Antonio, denouncing it as un-natural and therefore immoral, had been generally replaced by Shylock's pragmatic viewpoint.

We accept the regulation of the rate of interest as the basis for our modern monetary system. When the regulation is ignored, we have major problems.

Leverage: the physical principle

Why do we call it leverage? To visualize this, you may go back to your high school physics and remember a lever is a mechanical device that allows you to lift up a large weight with a minimum of exertion. There is usually a fixed support, a fulcrum, upon which the lever rests. The lever is often a straight, flat device, rather like a crowbar. One end of the lever is on the fulcrum, and the other end of the lever is under the object to be lifted. The weight that one can lift with the lever far exceeds the weight one could lift alone. It allows the human being to do what would not be humanly possible.

The cave man's discovery

R. Buckminster Fuller hypothesizes that man's first experience with leverage came when a cave man walked across a woods, stepped on a tree lying under two or three other trees, and observed that stepping on the lower tree lifted a higher tree:

> As he teetered he saw the third big tree lifting. It seemed impossible to him. He went over and tried using his own muscles to lift that great tree. He couldn't budge it. Then he climbed back atop the first smaller tree, purposefully teetering it, and surely enough it again elevated the larger tree.[4]

Because it was not "humanly possible" to lift the tree, the cave man, Fuller imagines, probably thought it was magic and erected it as a totem pole:

> It was probably a long time before he learned that any stout tree would do, and thus extracted the concept of the generalized principle of leverage out of all his earlier successive special-case experiences with such accidental discoveries. Only as he learned to generalize fundamental principles of physical universe did man learn to use his intellect effectively.[5]

Metaphysical application of the physical principle

We have come a long way from the cave man's tree, the original lever, to the ATM. In so doing, we once again establish the unique ability of man to observe physical principles and to give those principles metaphysical application. Fuller describes this generalization of physical principle:

> Once man comprehended that any tree would serve as a lever his intellectual advantages accelerated. Man freed of special-case superstition by intellect has had his survival potentials multiplied millions fold. By virtue of the leverage principles in gears, pulleys, transistors, and so forth, it is literally possible to do more with less in a multitude of physio-chemical ways. Possibly it was this intellectual augmentation of humanity's survival and success through the metaphysical perception of generalized principles which may be objectively employed that Christ was trying to teach in the obscurely told story of the loaves and the fishes.[6]

Man's power of reason: observation, application generalization

This is how man has mastered the physical universe. First he uses the physical principle, i.e. applies the lever to create gears, pulleys, transistors. He is able to do more with less exertion, to perform feats that are not humanly possible. As he observes the principle in action, he generalizes that principle, and then applies it somewhere else. That is the process of inductive reasoning: if this is true, and this is true, then this must be true. Man further masters the universe by taking the observed physical principles and applying them beyond the physical, metaphysically. We have used a rocket to launch a spacecraft to the moon through the observation, application, and generalization of physical principles. We have created the computer to leverage the action of the human brain and with that computer have linked the world through the internet. The enormous improvement in our way of life here on the planet in comfort and services results from the metaphysical application of the principle of leverage.

Bonds

Communities, states, nations, issue bonds for special projects: roads, bridges, parks. Sometimes the specific purpose for a bond is stated; sometimes it isn't. For instance, a city may sell a municipal bond to pay for new schools. The citizens buy the bonds at a discounted price, for less than the face value stated on the bond. When the bond matures, they will be repaid what they have paid plus whatever rate of interest the bond yields. This is a win/win situation. The city treasury takes in an influx of money to pay for the project. This means that the schools can be built immediately. The city does not have to wait until enough money is collected in taxes or from a special assessment. The citizen purchasing the bond has the security of the municipality standing behind the bond and a predictable yield on a stated date as return on the investment. The community as a whole enjoys the benefit of good schools to attract people to the community.

U.S. Treasuries

Our U.S. Treasury sells bonds, bills, and notes. During World War II, we sold "war bonds." People bought these bonds to pay for the war effort. As children we could buy stamps that we pasted in a book. The stamps cost ten cents each. When the book was filled, we had eighteen dollars worth of stamps. We could trade the book in for a bond that would mature in twenty-five years and would be worth twenty-five dollars. The Treasury bonds, bills, and notes sold today are not sold, as were those war bonds, for an express purpose. They are sold to fund the allocations in the national budget and to feed the deficit.

Homes

When the system is operating according to law and regulation, when we buy a home, we use leverage in our purchase. Our lever is the down payment, the small percentage of the price we pay at the time of purchase. The remainder of the purchase price, we borrow at a stated rate of interest. Think what a difference this has made in the quality of life. If we had to wait until we had saved the full amount to buy a home, how many people would own a home? Our mortgages provide us with instant gratification of the "American Dream."

When the system ignores law and regulation, as in the Sub-Prime Mortgage Crisis, we have leverage "gone awry." Ordinary citizens thought they were buying capital assets, homes, when banks were offering anyone a mortgage without down payments or proof of income at low interest rates, adjustable to higher rates, predicted on the assumption the price of houses would continue to climb. Some mortgage companies were even offering 110% or 120% financing based on the assumption of rising home values. The public became caught up in an elaborate mental game created by bankers who skirted the law and ignored regulation. See *The Big Short*.

The financial system's abuse of the generalized principle of leverage is "Leverage gone awry." The U.S. government's abuse of the generalized principle of leverage is "Leverage gone amuck." This does not detract from the incredible importance of purposeful application of this principle to promote human endeavor, to empower mankind to do "more with less," and to improve the quality of our lives – my reason for writing this chapter.

The loaves and the fishes

Fuller says that the story about Jesus and the loaves and the fishes might have been Christ's way of teaching the metaphysical generalization of the physical principle of leverage. Let's explore the basis for that remark. In the story of the loaves and the fishes, Jesus is said to have fed a multitude with five loaves and two fishes. If you recall the story, Jesus had been with a multitude of 5000 people for an entire day. As evening approached, his disciples urged him to send the multitude away so that they could go to the villages to buy food.

> But Jesus said unto them, They need not depart; give ye them to eat.
> And they say unto him, We have here but five loaves, and two fishes.
> He said, Bring them hither to me.
> And he commanded the multitude to sit down on the grass and took the five loaves and the two fishes, and looking up toheaven, he blessed, and brake, and gave the loaves to his disciples, and the disciples to the multitude.
> And they did all eat, and were filled: and they took up the fragments that remained twelve baskets full.
> And they that had eaten were about five thousand men, besides women and children.
>
> Matthew: 16-21

Expectation, Belief, Word

In this account, as in the account of many of the activities of Jesus as documented by Matthew, Mark, Luke, and John, he demonstrates the power of the mind to determine the reality. This is true with his healings; this is true with his "miracles." This mental power is unlimited. Jesus' stories are all stories of Jesus taking the natural resources, wherever they are, be it a human body, a vessel of water, or the contents of a lunch bag, and transforming them by his *Expectation, Belief, and Word*. What is an *expectation*? "*Ex*" means out. *Spectare* means to look at, a derivation of *specere*, to see. So an expectation is just a looking out for, just as we look out for someone coming down the road. And what is a *belief*. Now "*bi*" means complete, "*lief*" goes back to Middle English "*bileafe*" and the Old English "*geleafa*", with a consistent meaning of acceptance of the truth of anything without certain proof; i.e. a mental conviction. We don't get too far in the dictionary with *word*: "A linguistic form that can meaningfully be spoken in isolation." You will recall that Fuller considers the *word* as the first industrial tool, i.e. a tool that is used by two or more. The first use of a symbolic sound as a means of communication became an industrial tool.

The power of the spoken word

Let us go back to the first chapter of Genesis to explore *word*. We are told this about the creation:

> In the beginning God created the heaven and the earth.
> And the earth was without form and void; and darkness was upon the face of the deep. And the spirit of God moved upon the face of the waters.
> And God said, Let there be light: and there was Light.
>
> Genesis: 1-3

As the act of creation is described, it has two parts: what God "says," his *word*, and what he "calls" what he has created i.e. "And God saw the light, that it was good: and God divided the light from the darkness. And God called the light Day, and the darkness he called Night." Nothing existed until God spoke it into existence, and it had no identity until God called it something, gave it a name. God had the *Expectation*, the *Belief*, and the *Word*. This is exactly the procedure Jesus follows as well. In Jesus' act of creation, or of <u>re</u>creation, as in turning water to wine or five loaves and two fishes into food for thousands, he acts upon the creative medium, whatever material he has before him with: 1) the *Expectation*; 2) the *Belief*, and 3) the *Word*. *Expectation*s, *Belief*s, and *Word*s are not packaged and sold at WalMart. They are not available on the shelves of Home Depot. Grocers do not stock these items in the produce section or keep them in the freezer. They are metaphysical commodities.

Free metaphysical commodities

Indeed, *these metaphysical commodities are totally free.* We can have as many of them, as much of them, as we choose. They are available to us every second of every minute of every hour of every day. They are without measurement, without quantification, without limit. If we *expect*, *believe*, and *speak*, and then apply the "elbow grease," it will be. You will recall its effectiveness in realizing the "Big Picture." And it will be. We can do what God did; we can do what Jesus did. We do, in fact, unconsciously practice the same methodology every day; and we also accept the gifts of those who unconsciously utilize this methodology as a part of their daily business.

No restriction on your possibility

My intent is to make you, the reader, conscious of this methodology so that you can draw on the unlimited ability of the Universe to respond to your *Expectation*, *Belief*, and *Word*. This explanation corroborates the truth that nothing in the Universe exists except thought and energy. That is the extraordinary message of leverage.   Since God or Universe is the big thinker who thought it up, and since you uniquely have the ability to retrace the pattern of God's thinking, you have absolutely no restriction upon your possibility. We can create everything we need through *Expectation*, *Belief*, and *Word* plus Work. This procedure demonstrates what man has already been able to create by generalizing upon an idea, the *idea*, originated in the physical image of the bottom tree lifting up the top tree. From it, we have produced a world of items, comforts, services, and agencies.

Promises and equivalents of exchange

Free promises

Man's culture evolved outward from the single individual, family to tribe to inter-tribal communication and exchange. Think of him as the "great pirate" who had the courage to get into his canoe, travel from island to island, and discover the unique goods and services available there. He placed himself in the center, as the know-it-all of exchange, the ultimate power figure because he could get anybody anything. This early exchange was by barter. Man eventually observed that the barter system was cumbersome. After a while it got to be too much trouble to carry a cow to someone in exchange for fifty bushels of grain, so he invented a way to promise an equivalent, i.e. you owe me the worth of a cow in grain. Note that *promises are free.*

Promise of equivalence

When man began to dig in the earth, he came up with something shiny and scarce and for a long time, he tied the "promise of equivalence" to the metal he found in the ground: gold. This created more and better pirates, along with bankers, and thieves, considered in some circles as synonymous entities. But man, representative of the general population, didn't really care, so long as he could get his meat and potatoes. The precious nature of gold required variations in value, so for many centuries, man took other metals and used them as a medium of exchange, placing numerical values on "promises of equivalence," which worked so long as no one questioned the promise. Gold was always the bottom line, so we would say, to express this in words, that something was "as good as gold."

When man got to the point that he needed more "promises of equivalence" than he had gold, he did away with the gold and just issued the promise, a piece of paper that states, "In God we trust." A promise is expressed in words. In 1972, an American president, Richard Nixon, took the United States monetary system off the gold standard. We no longer required parity between the amount of gold we had on reserve and the number of promises we had issued, i.e. money. Maynard Keynes always considered the gold standard a "barbaric" practice anyway.

As good as gold

Women continued to go to the supermarket to buy groceries, men continued to go to the hardware store to buy trinkets to fix things, and car manufacturers continued to turn automobiles off the assembly line, all because we had been trained over the centuries to accept the promise because it was "as good as gold." And so it is. So long as man accepts the promise, it really doesn't matter exactly what is behind it. We don't even think to ask. We trust the system.

The American Dream

A home

The reason the United States of America has the highest standard of living in the world is because it has the most sophisticated way of using *Expectation*, *Belief*, and *Word*. We began in the 1940s to articulate the American dream: a house for every family, a chicken in every pot, and a car in every driveway. We made that idea a reality with another idea, a mortgage for the house, and a loan for the car, letting the bottom tree, a little tree, lift up a great big tree. So to buy a house, we put a little bit down, and we go to the bank to get the rest. The bank takes our pieces of paper and our coins, issues another piece of paper, a contract, on which words are written, and we sign the contract.

Then we spend, theoretically, at least at the beginning, the rest of our lives, thirty years, paying back the bank. Bear in mind that it was very common for the American male to be dead at fifty or sixty when the American mortgage came into being. The average male in the 1960s would retire, pick up nine Social Security checks, and then die before 65.

A car

To buy a car we did the same thing we did to buy a house. We went to the bank and showed the bank that we had a little bit of money, i.e. currency, to put down on the purchase of a car. The bank took the currency and the car, pronounced them all the possession of the bank, and issued a contract, a piece of paper on which words are recorded. The bank then gave the manufacturer of the car a copy of the contract and a portion of the currency. The manufacturer then distributed currency to his employees, which they, in turn, took to the store to buy food for their families and took to the bank to buy houses and cars for themselves.

Ownership in the mind

An extraordinary thing takes place in the human mind when the coins, pieces of paper, and the words are thus exchanged, the promise of equivalence. The house, which actually belongs to the bank, in our minds becomes our house. We paint it, carpet it, landscape it, clean it, furnish it. We become citizens of our neighborhood. We go to the polls, and we vote to issue bonds for schools and parks and roads, because we are home-owners and we want our communities to be fine places to live. We take our car to the service station and change the oil. We wash the car, park it in the garage, and drive it carefully so as not to bang it up, because it is our car. The principle of owner-ship brings out the best in human nature, even though it may only be a combination of partial ownership and an idea based upon *Expectation*, *Belief*, and *Word*, a "promise of equivalence."

Fed funds: more promises

As the banks needed more and more paper and coins to empower Americans to have the idea of ownership, we created another idea. For every one piece of paper on deposit in the bank, assume $1 each, the federal government would let the bank have ten pieces of paper, $10. Initially, the federal government had as much gold on deposit as it issued in paper, the "promise of equivalence." When it needed more promises than it had gold, it kept the promise. It did not really matter so long as the government made the promise, and we accepted the promise.

Exchange based on promises and expectation

In fact, we have a world of exchange based on *promises* which are free. We act on *Expectation* of promises, as Keynes observed of the entrepreneur: "Meanwhile, the entrepre-neur {including both the producer and the investor in this description} has to form the best expectations he can as to what the consumers will be prepared to pay when he is ready to supply them... after the elapse of what may be a lengthy period and he has no choice but to be guided by these expectations, if he is to produce at all by processes which occupy time."

So long as we have the *Expectation*, the *Belief* and the *Word*, we really don't need anything else. This is how we went from being out of money, the Great Depression, to having enough money to wage World War II. Our system of free enterprise is an extension of both the metaphysical principle of leverage and the metaphysical practice exemplified by Jesus. There is absolutely no limit to what the mind of man can create out of the metaphysical. Actually, the only reality is the mind. The only limitation you have upon you is how you use your mind, how you direct and use your thoughts.

Leverage and daily practice

What can leverage mean for you in your daily practice, in your business, in your work. It is always the principle of *doing more with less*. The computer is a form of leverage. The program in the computer replicates the function of the human brain. We could alphabetize all the listings in the telephone book for the city of San Francisco by sorting them according to the letters of the alphabet, and then within each letter, sorting and organizing. It might take us several months. The computer is programmed to do that for us. One program is written; it is used by millions of people; each person using it does more with less. That is why Bill Gates and Steve Jobs became so rich.

Computer software is a metaphysical lever. The Internet is the next extension of that leverage.

Never in the history of man has leverage been used so successfully to empower so many. Thousands of people have become millionaires, and some have become billionaires because of the technology based on intellectual property. The access to knowledge on the planet has been transformed by this use of leverage, with critical impact for all areas of life: home, business, schools, public institutions, government, private and religious institutions. No one has remained untouched.

The Silicon Valley companies assemble the brightest and best minds to solve problems and to create products that reflect those solutions. The public considers the intent of Microsoft and its leader to be benign. When I challenge young people to create the biggest picture they can for their lives, the computer whizzes want to work for Microsoft or Apple or Facebook or Google and receive stock options. It used to be when a kid grew up, he wanted to be president. Today, he *and* she want to be Bill Gates, Mark Zuckerberg, Larry Page, Sheryl Sandberg.

Elon Musk, CEO of TESLA and SpaceX brilliantly uses leverage. He pre-sold his most recent model of TESLA before it has even gone into production and infused his company with needed capital. The huge plant he is building in Reno will produce battery packs for both his cars and his Powerwall batteries. The Powerwall batteries, combined with Solar panels, will store energy during the day to be used for free at night. Musk believes this innovation can eventually replace the huge carbon-producing power plants. He just negotiated to purchase the solar company to make the solar panels. How smart is that!

Films, TV, radio

A single movie is produced, copies are distributed to theaters, and thousands of people can see it the first weekend. After the movie has completed its run in the theaters, it is recorded on DVD, streamed on NetFlix or Amazon Prime.   Movies are frozen in time, permanent works of art. It is amazing to reflect on the fear of scarcity thinking: initially it was feared television would do away with radio. Then television was considered a threat to the film industry. Then the VCR was considered a threat to the movie theaters. Leverage actually augments opportunities. When we learn to *do more with less*, we create more avenues for participation and for consumption.

Books, CD's, t-shirts, posters, and prints

Every time you purchase a book, a CD, a print, a poster, or a logo t-shirt, you are consuming a leveraged product. I am using leverage right now. This book can be printed and re-printed, and there is no limit to the number of copies that can be sold. A single concert may be played for a thousand people, but when recorded and sold as CD's or on ITunes, it reaches millions. A single t-shirt design can be printed on a million t-shirts. When posters and prints are made of a beautiful picture, it can be enjoyed by millions.   The Khan Academy has revolutionized the teaching of basic concepts, accessible from anywhere in the world on-line and free.

Leverage opportunities limitless

You can think leverage. You can think about how you can take what you are doing, a single effort, and how you can replicate that. If you're engaged in work or a profession where you can't see an application for leverage, think about how you might modify your endeavors to employ leverage. When you conceive of yourself as self-employed, when you acknowledge that only thought and energy exist, then there is no limit to your possibility. If Jack Ma can create Alibaba, the largest on-line retailer in the world, without understanding how the internet works, how can you harness the technology exploding around you exponentially. What can you sell? The message of all great motivators is that there is no limit to what we can achieve through our thought.

A man is like a bit of Labrador spar, which has no lustre as you turn it in your hand until you come to a particular angle; then it shows deep and beautiful colors. There is no adaptation or universal applicability in men, but each has his special talent, and the mastery of successful men consists in adroitly keeping themselves where and when that turn shall oftenest to be practised.

Emerson, "Experience" [1]

If our young men miscarry in their first enterprises, they lose all heart. If the young merchant fails, men say he is ruined. If the finest genius studies at one of our colleges and is not installed in an office within one year afterwards in the cities or suburbs of Boston or New York it seems to his friends and to himself that he is right in being disheartened and in complaining the rest of his life. A sturdy lad from New Hampshire or Vermont, who in turn tries all the professions, who teams it, farms it, peddles, keeps a school, preaches, edits a newspaper, goes to Congress, buys a township, and so forth, in successive years, and always like a cat falls on his feet, is worth a hundred of these city dolls. He walks abreast with his days and feels no shame in not 'studying a profession,' for he does not postpone his life, but lives already.

Emerson, "Self Reliance" [2]

SYNERGY

A typical office setting: "Bartelby the Scrivener"

HERMAN MELVILLE'S STORY "Bartelby the Scrivener: A story of Wall Street" is narrated by a lawyer who describes himself thus:

> I am a man who, from his youth upwards, has been filled with a profound conviction that the easiest way of life is the best. Hence, though I belong to a profession prover-bially energetic and nervous, even to turbulence, at times, yet nothing of that sort have I ever suffered to invade my peace. I am one of the unambitious lawyers who never addresses a jury, or in any way draws down public applause; but, in the cool tranquility of a snug retreat, do a snug business among rich men's bonds, and mortgages, and title-deeds. All who know me, consider me an emi-nently safe man. The late John Jacob Astor, a personage little given to poetic enthusiasm had no hesitation in pro-nouncing my first grand point to be prudence; my next method. [3]

Turkey

This lawyer employs a staff of three in his office: Turkey, Nippers, and Ginger Nut. Turkey is named because of his face which glows red at the beginning of the workday, blazes by noon, and then settles to a burning coal by 6:00 p.m. He is a man about sixty years old, apt to be altogether too energetic, with a "strange, inflamed, flurried, flighty recklessness of activity about him." He is a good worker until lunch time; and then he falls apart, not only blotting the documents he copies in the afternoon, but also making a racket with his chair. He spills his sand-box, impatiently splits his pens "all to pieces" when he mends them, then in anger throws the pens on the floor "in a sudden passion" and leans over his table, "boxing his papers about in a most indecorous manner." He is rash, insolent, and subject to habitual temper tantrums. Although the lawyer prefers for Turkey not to work at all in the afternoon, Turkey insists upon it.

Nippers

These two older men in the office, the lawyer and Turkey, both "somewhere not far from sixty," are accompanied by two younger ones, Nippers and Ginger Nut. Nippers, a young man of 25, is the "victim of two evil powers – ambition and indigestion." He is definitely a candidate for ulcers: "The ambition was evinced by a certain impatience of the duties of a mere copyist, an unwarrantable usurpation of strictly professional affairs, such as the original drawing up of legal documents. The indigestion seemed betokened in an occasional nervous testiness and grinning irritability, causing the teeth to audibly grind together over mistakes committed in copying; unnecessary maledictions, hissed, rather than spoken."

Ginger Nut

Young Ginger Nut, a mere lad of 12, has been sent to the lawyer as an apprentice. He is a quick learner for whom "the whole noble science of the law was contained in a nut shell." Ginger Nut has earned his name by running a particular errand for Turkey and Nippers: "They sent Ginger Nut frequently for that peculiar cake – small, flat, round, and very spicy – after which he had been named by them." ("Ginger nut" is a British term; today, in the United States, we call the "ginger nut" a "ginger snap.") Turkey gets so carried away with eating Ginger Nuts in the afternoon that once he sealed a mortgage with one moistened between his lips.

Bartelby

When the lawyer receives a big contract requiring more copying than Turkey and Nippers are capable of performing, he hires Bartelby, "Pallidly neat, pitiably respectable, incurably forlorn." Bartelby works carefully, both day and night, "silently, palely, mechanically," and the lawyer would have been pleased with his diligence, had Bartelby been cheerful about it. But he was not cheerful about anything. Furthermore, Bartelby will not participate in the proofreading of his work. Whenever asked to do it, Bartelby replies, "I would prefer not to." Bartelby secretly takes up residence in the office, never leaving. Eventually, he, by his obstinacy, takes such control over the lawyer that the lawyer is forced to move his office elsewhere to get away from him.

Prefer not to

By the time they move, the word "prefer" has preferential status in all of their vocabularies, demonstrating Bartelby's profound influence. The new tenant can't move in because Bartelby is still there. When the old landlord, after pleas and threats, cannot get Bartelby to leave the premises, he asks the lawyer to intervene. The lawyer has no moral suasion whatsoever with Bartelby. The landlord calls the authorities, and finally Bartelby is carried off to prison where he "prefers not to" eat, and he dies. The lawyer describes him in his final fetal position: "Strangely huddled at the base of the wall, his knees drawn up, and lying on his side, his head touching the cold stones, I saw the wasted Bartelby."

Typical office dysfunction

This office drama may exaggerate what you have experienced, but perhaps not. We often find ourselves working at jobs where we blot in the afternoon, fuss and fidget, grind our teeth, hiss at our co-workers, have ambition to be the boss, run errands when instead we could be running the whole operation, and express "I would prefer not to, not in words, then in deeds. Certainly, I have worked in many offices similarly dysfunctional; and I, too, have even performed dysfunctionally.

When I think back upon it, the source of the dysfunction is a mismatch of temperament and skills with the assigned job.

The old man in the kitchen

It reminds me of the Swedish folk tale about the old man who worked in the forest, chopping wood and burning char- coal. He grew jealous of his old woman who merely sat at home cooking porridge, eating, and enjoying herself, or so he thought. The old woman, sick of his bickering, finally agreed to switch jobs. When the old woman returned from the forest with a big bundle of firewood on her back, she found her house in utter chaos: the dog had eaten the bacon; the bread had burned; the beer had run out of the barrel; the cream and the churn had fallen in the spring; her jacket was chopped for greens and cooked in the pot; the cow was hanged in the chimney; and the old man was burned and bruised. The old man discovered that domestic engineering requires multi-task capability, something women have naturally and men would probably "prefer not to." The old man cheerfully went back to the forest the next day.

Mismatched employment

Mismatching costs the employer and frustrates the employee. My first such experience occurred during the sum- mer between completing my B.A. degree and starting work on my M.A. It was the first summer I hadn't gone home to work on my family's golf course. Through a friend I found a job as a typist at the Continuing Education Center of the School of

Public Health. My boss, Ann Murphy, a quiet, orderly woman, a librarian by education, was in charge of coordinating conferences and then editing, printing, and disseminating the papers and speeches given in the conference meetings. To let you know how long ago this was, let me just say my pay was $2.25 an hour and the typing was done on typewriters without correction tape. A word processor or computer, if in existence, probably would have occupied a whole building. Correction tape, if invented, was not in common use, i.e. we didn't have any. Had there been "white out," it would have been forbidden.

At first Ann assigned me to type letters. She required that they be typed perfectly, without error. For the first two weeks, each day I went the whole day and never completed a single letter. Just as Turkey did, I blotted. I was afraid I'd get fired and not be able to pay my rent, and that just made my typing worse. Ann, the soul of resourcefulness and patience, not to have me undone by mechanical devices, hit upon another idea. She set me up with earphones to transcribe the tapes from the conferences. It didn't matter if I made mistakes in the transcription. Then after I transcribed the tapes, she let me re-write the speeches and edit them for publication. Since I was an English major and enjoyed writing, this worked perfectly. I kept the job the whole year that I did my Master's degree, coming and going around my classes because my work didn't require a set schedule. She turned the letter typing over to the other two "girls" in the office, one a Chemistry major who always did everything perfectly, and the other, the mother of two small children who was absolutely meticulous. We were as snug as a bug in a rug. Our office was humming along synergistically.

Synergy common nomenclature

When R. Buckminster Fuller began to talk to university audiences about synergy in the 1960's and 70's, it was a new term. The book he wrote, *Synergetics*, appealed to his own specialized audience accustomed to unwinding the convolutions of his style and syntax. "Synergy" is now common nomenclature. Stephen Covey made it one of his "seven habits" of effective people in his book by that name. When I opened the Orange County South telephone book this morning and turned to the "syn" in the Business section, I found: Synergistic Electronic Systems, Synergistic Solutions, Synergy Computer Consultation, Synergy Electronics, Synergy Food Service Consultants, Synergy Staffing Inc, and Synergy Wellness Center. We thus see from this small sample the use of the term "synergy" in everything from electronics and computer networks to temp agencies and nutrition.

The toenail: no predictor

The early definition used by Fuller was that the behavior of wholes could not be predicted by the behavior of any one part, just as the toenail would not predict the whole body. When he made that analogy in 1963, he wasn't thinking about DNA. Certainly a toenail does not look like the whole body. It is appropriate, however, when presenting the concept of synergy, to use the human body, for it operates according to cooperating and simultaneously functioning systems. Fundamental to Fuller's thought is his analysis of systems and his incredible respect for the geometrical, mathematical, overlapping, cooperating systemization of the universe.

The work of Deepak Chopra has made us even more sensitive to the perfection of the human system. Indeed, one might say that the systematic functioning of the human has become the paradigm for industry, for organizations, for marketing. When we are in perfect health, aware and accepting of ourselves, then we are functioning perfectly; and the chances are better for all that follows to function perfectly: the relationships, the family, the schools, the community, the nation, and the world.

Dysfunction: system awry

We have also come to a greater awareness that, unless we pay attention, we may spend most of our lives compensating in one way or another for the dysfunctionality of our parents, our families, our spouses, our social experiences, our work experiences. The word dysfunction assumes something in the system is awry, working improperly, one part throwing off the desired state, the perfect functioning of the system as a whole. To define and direct our experience, we must know why we think the way we do, why we accepted the attitudes and beliefs that affect our thinking. Only then can we understand how we got ourselves where we are. This gives us a choice: We can get off the hamster wheel and *reset, reboot,* and *replant.* Most of us assume we have only this voyage to set things straight. For those who believe we come back, the work of Brian L. Weiss, M.D., author of *Many Lives, Many Masters,* suggests we bring back what we failed to set in order, and it continues to upset the apple cart until we do.

A game of fortune?

We can effectively use the concept of synergy to address our choice, to figure out how to get out of the mess we're in or how to make the best of it. When we know the make-up of our particular cog in the wheel of fortune we have created for ourselves, we can love it or leave it. Fortune, *Fortuna*, usually bears the connotation of something good, or at least is conceived that way in our climate of opinion or our race consciousness. One goes off to make one's fortune. One plays the Wheel of Fortune to win prizes and a moment of glory. One buys lottery tickets. I actually sold a house to a woman who won the California lottery. In *Death of a Salesman*, Willie Loman's brother, Ben, headed for Alaska, was confused and turned around, and ended up in Africa, the Gold Coast. He tells Willie's sons, "Why, boys, when I was seventeen I walked into the jungle, and when I was twenty-one I walked out. And by God I was rich."

Thrown off!

A world-renowned astrologer, at least his fee supported the reputation that he was world-renowned, once did my chart. He said, "You have Jupiter in your first house. What this means is that Jupiter can take you up to the highest pinnacle, but he can also throw you off." Being "thrown off," unfortunately, is the other side of fortune. How many times have we all been "thrown off": thrown off in our health, thrown off in our job, thrown off in our relationships? We have a tendency when that happens to blame ourselves, and yet we very well may have been "thrown off" for a reason. Sometimes we have to be "thrown" to force us "to get back on our feet." Our folk language of old sayings certainly supports our experience. Sally Jesse Raphael, a popular television host for seventeen years, was fired eighteen times.

Back on our feet

I have found the concept of synergy can serve us effectively as a way to come to understand ourselves so we can make wise decisions. No matter whom we wish to blame for the result, however we have turned out to be is the way we are. If we can accept and bless the result, then we have a chance to work with it effectively. If we fight it, then we will get "thrown off" in one way or another. There are a myriad of reasons we may not like the way we are: Mother expected better of me; I didn't pursue my father's profession; I'm not making enough money, I don't have enough education, I never got the opportunities my siblings did; just as I was about to make it, the economy or the market or real estate went all to hell. We have heard them all and used our excuse of choice. Actually, whatever happened shaped you and made you who you are. *Reset, reboot, replant.*

Quality functioning

My focus here on the concept of synergy will be personalized, directing our attention not on quality circles in an industrial setting, but on quality functioning at work, at home, and in life in general. The work of Richard Deming, rejected by our automobile makers at the end of World War II, was adopted by General MacArthur when he was charged with rebuilding Japan. Deming went there to teach the Japanese how to involve the entire team of contributors to the finished product in the design of the system to make and market that product, thus creating synergy.

The input of the worker on the assembly line was equally as important as that of the designer, the engineer and the director of marketing. The quality circles established an equalitarian acceptance of personal contribution and inspired a self-loving participation from each individual involved in the enterprise. Japan emerged with better cars than we were making in the U.S., and it sent our auto industry in the tank. We recovered our market share when we, too, adopted Deming's ideas and methodology.

As an aside, the auto industry, indicative of the manufacturing segment of the U.S. economy, has continued to move away from the expertise of the synergetically performing enterprise to "easier" paths to profits. Rama Foroohar's new book, *Makers and Takers: The Rise of Finance and the Fall of American Business*, demonstrates how the "financialization" of banking and of business in general has hampered real growth and innovation. The result is an "upside-down" economy where finance, rather than serving as a catalyst, has become the end product – a dangerous path following a financial crisis fueled by excessive debt and credit and a smoke-and-mirrors recovery.

She points out that while finance makes up only 7% of the economy and creates only 4% of the jobs, it generates more than a fourth of corporate profits.[4]

Up close and personal: DISC

We can't change industry, but we can change our focus and ourselves. My personalized approach to synergy is meant to give you a similar sense of the importance of your special contribution and to inspire self-love. We will get up close and personal. The quality circles in all aspects of your life generate outward from your center. You know that center by knowing yourself. You are at peace and harmony with the person you are when you can bless and accept your part in the grand design. As we go through the following process, you have permission to let go of judgment of yourself, and to let go of judgment of others as well. It will prepare you to *replant.*

The model I am using here is called the **DISC**,[5] and it is the basis of a psychological test used to build "high performance teams" or to determine aptitude for specific professions. It is a model that defines people by four factors, each of us tending to have a predominance in one of them, usually accompanied by at least a smattering of each of the four. The test determines the predominant factor by asking questions about preference, experience, and preferred solutions to challenges and situations. It is carefully constructed so that you can't outguess or manipulate your answers toward a preferred result.

Other psychological tests,[6] for instance the Briggs-Stratton, give similar information. Bear in mind as we go over these four personality types that we come in all sorts of mixtures, and harmonies, and balances. Yet each of us can probably find a predominance within one category and relate to it more specifically. Since the results of the test are placed on a graph, the predominate factor appears at the top of the graph and is therefore called "high." You will be "high" in one area and "low" or in the middle in the other areas.

D: Desire to direct and dominate other people. This personality type is egocentric, demanding, determined, driving, competitive, ambitious, creative, pioneering, opinionated, forceful, and decisive. The person who is high in **D** is likely to be an entrepreneur or to undertake whatever he does in an entrepreneurial manner. If he goes into real estate, he'll go with ReMax, a real estate firm made up of independent agents, rather than joining Berkshire Hathaway or Coldwell Banker, firms with a strong corporate identity. He will create Apple in his garage. If he is a great teacher promoted to administration, he will go crazy in the bureaucracy and will either end up as president or out, i.e. thrown out. You don't need more than one high **D** at the head of a company, an organization, or a family. In fact, I once worked for a company headed by a husband and wife who were both high **D**'s. They spent every meeting arguing with each other, over-rode each other's decisions, and the company finally went under. It was embarrassing for employees to witness the exchange between them. I often wondered how confusing it must have been to their child.

I: Intuitive need to interact with other people. This personality type is warm, persuasive, optimistic, cheerful, caring, giving, empathetic, sympathetic, enthusiastic, and often political and jockeying for position, to the point of being effusive. If you go to a party with this personality, on the way home she will define each of the people she met with the statement, "He really liked me." The person high in **I** considers being liked as the most important thing in the world. She is likely to wear a necklace or bracelet or pin with her name on it. You knew her in high school because she would walk down the hall saying "Hi, how are you," to everyone, always running for Homecoming Queen. You may go to her with your problems because you know she cares. A high **I** may be good in sales, because you like her, but she'll need some high **D** as well to close. Never put a high **I** on an assembly line because she'll talk all the time and distract the other employees.

S: Takes pleasure in serving others. This person is a team player, result-oriented, dependable, takes direction well, reliable, patient, resistant to change, predictable, consistent, steady, stable, deliberate, passive. We rely on this person to open the store in the morning and to close it at night. We know that whatever we ask this person to do, he will do it. He never argues with you, never tries to outshine you, is willing to walk in your shadow and to make you feel important. The people high in **S** are needed in numbers by any effective organization, for they are the people who perform the tasks that need to be done to bring a product to market, to bring the goods for the bake sale, to keep the soccer team in clean uniforms and on the field. The high **S**'s are the backbone of any enterprise.

C: Complies with the highest standards of excellence. This person is so self-critical and so self-demanding of accuracy that he is never finished with his research, never has quite completed his task, because he worries he may have missed something. He is intelligent, careful, cautious, indecisive, exacting, balanced, systematic, neat, and tactful. You know that this person will evade giving strong opinions because he will see both sides of the issue, will never quite complete his deliberation. You want this person in research, in accounting, in financial analysis and economic forecasting, in engineering, in any area of an organization where a better solution may be found to a problem. It's important that the person high in **C** be able to stay in the background.

Each valuable

Each of these personality types and the various combinations of them contribute to the success of any enterprise. The most important issue is determining which personality type should be doing which task. You would not ask a person high in **C** to do public relations, or sales, or to act as the CEO of an organization. This personality wishes to be anonymous. You might place a person high in **S** in customer service, but only if it is balanced with **I**. You would not ask a high **S** to do telemarketing sales, especially out-bound, because she would freeze and never be able to pick up the telephone. You might place a high **D** in sales, in upper management, but you would never place him on an assembly line or in your research division. You would place your high **I** in human resources, or sales, or public relations, but not in management or research. As a manager, being liked would take precedence over getting the job done.

Know yourself.

If you think back over your life, you may observe how often you have been misplaced or have been asked to do things contrary to your nature. I speak from my own experience. I didn't know that as a teacher I was an entrepreneur until I got promoted to administration, drove myself and everyone around me crazy, and then was thrown out. Please know how many years it has taken for me to come to this realization, to be able to talk about, and to be able to accept and bless it. At the time I thought it meant the end of everything that I had educated and trained myself to do. For the next decade, as I punished myself in guilt for being a failure, to earn a living I was forced to explore fields that welcomed my personality type, *sales*: particularly stocks and bonds and real estate.

All part of whole

We carry with us from one time of life to another, from one work to another, all we have learned and all we have experienced. I approach my business as a teacher, counselor, listener, and closer. That's where a balance between the high **I** and high **D** for me is so crucial. The first time I took this test, I was off the chart as a high **D** with no high **I**. It was the high **D** out of control that moved me to the next phase of my life.

Improve and understand relationships

The **DISC** categories are useful in personal relationships. People who stay married for fifty or sixty years usually complement each other rather than conflict. It is possible that two high **D**'s might be attracted to each other and might even stay with each other because of the challenge. Chances are, however, the need to be in charge will lead them to conflict. Here are two marriages.

The doctor and the High S

My father-in-law was a medical doctor and surgeon. He had tremendous high **D** at home and in the operating room and high **I** at the office when he interacted with patients. My mother-in-law was cheerful, with some high **I**, but she was predominately high **S**. She called my father-in-law "Doctor," ironed his socks as well as sheets and tablecloths on a mangle; and her pantry was perfectly ordered, with even each kind of soup carefully matched and stacked together.

My mother-in-law had always "appeared" to be strong and decisive because she was outspoken. She always had opinions about issues and exercised leadership in her community. She and her husband had traveled together, building their trips around meetings of the International College of Surgeons. She had loved the travel, and I thought after his death she would travel again and recreate her life. On the contrary, it was as if she lost her identity when she lost him, and she became a recluse. She had identity as a doctor's wife, but not as an independent individual.

The farmer and his wife

My maternal grandmother, on the other hand, was a complete surprise to her family. She bore ten children, worked side by side with my grandfather in the farm fields, rode with him in the truck to market, waited on him "hand and foot," and took care of the house with whatever energy she had left, all high **S** activity. I saw her as a worn-out, overweight, farm-woman in a flowered house dress with run-down oxfords and varicose veins. When we were children, she would scare us if we were naughty by saying she would get her "dander up," and she would drop her false teeth; so I also considered her pretty mean and ugly, too. I can still visualize with horror her face with the dropping teeth by the light of a kerosene lantern.

When my grandfather died in his early sixties, my first discovery was the poetry and art and beauty in the soul of my grandmother. Her sister came for the funeral, and they recited poetry by memory for hour after hour. After the funeral, my grandmother dyed her hair back to its original auburn, bought new clothes, began to paint in watercolors and oils, learned to drive a car, and traveled around the country visiting her children and grandchildren. In retrospect, I see how much of her true personality, her high **I** she stuffed away and subordinated in her marriage to my very demanding high **D** German/Austrian grandfather who expected servitude from his wife and children. In retrospect, I should have heard it in the melodic tone of her voice inherited by several of her children, although certainly not in my demanding mother.

Misplacement destructive

Although we can cultivate aspects of our personality that we wish to develop and can exercise a degree of control over our relationships, this is not always the case with our work. It is important to avoid totally inappropriate work for our predominant personality type. Here is a flagrant and painful example of misplacement for a family I encountered in California. The father was a violinist and had held the equivalence to a tenured position in the Boston Symphony. His wife had held a research position with AT&T in Boston. When AT&T downsized, rather than giving her a golden handshake, she was transferred to California and placed in the sales division. Because they had two college-age children, and her income was higher, the husband gave up his position in the orchestra and followed her. When I met them they had one child at USC and one at Berkeley. The husband had been unable to find a position as a musician and felt dejected and depressed. He was doing telemarketing, hated it and hated himself.

Within six months the wife failed to meet her sales quotas and was terminated. AT&T must have known, should have known, that a research scientist would not succeed in sales. The research scientist, to be successful, is predominately high in **C**, the opposite of the successful high **D**, high **I** sales personality. This family was cruelly disrupted and subjected to frustration and sorrow because of corporate decisions made without taking behavior factors into consideration. Or perhaps the corporation did take these factors into consideration and used this as a method to get rid of an employee with seniority without the cost of the "golden handshake." Had the wife in this instance a better understanding of her predominant personality type, she would not have accepted the sales job and would have looked elsewhere for a similar research position.

Correct balance effective

On the other hand, here is an example of a large pharmaceutical company taking advantage of sensitivity to personality types. This involves a brilliant young research scientist with a doctorate degree in Micro-Cellular-Developmental Biology, a definite high **C**. Before taking a position with a major chemical-pharmaceutical research company, he worked as a post-doctoral student at Stanford for three years, doing genetic research on myopia by studying *drosophila*, fruit flies. He is meticulous, careful, and methodical. He is assigned to a research team within the company designated to determine the feasibility of a new drug.

He complains there is a woman assigned to his team who acts as a "tattle-tale," always reporting to the top management about their results before they are ready for anyone to know about them. This corporation has wisely and prudently placed a person high in **I** and **D** on this research team of people high in **C**. The **C**'s alone would never be finished, would never have results to share, because their research would never be quite done. This young man, incidentally, is married to a high **D**. They complement each other. In fact, in charting the results of the **DISC** test, a person high in both **D** and **C** has the "millionaire's curve," the ability to do the research and then take it to market.

The Right Questions:

Strengths?

How often have you been through an annual review with your supervisor or manager and emerged with a list of things you need to work on, the areas where you are weak. How much better it would be for the organization as a whole if each person's strengths were to be supported and developed, and their weak areas compensated by someone strong in those areas.

A tool similarly useful as the DISC is the Gallup *Strength Finder*. [7] Gallup surveyed 10 million people on the topic of how productive people are at work. Only one-third agreed with the statement, "At work, I have the opportunity to do what I do best every day." They found that of the people who disagreed with or strongly disagreed with this statement, not a single person was emotionally engaged on the job. In contrast, they found that people who have the opportunity to focus on their strengths are six times as likely to be engaged in their jobs and three times as likely to report having an excellent quality of life in general.

Gallup's *Strengths Finder 2.0* uses 34 themes to classify and measure "talent."

Each book comes with an on-line assessment. You have 20 seconds to respond to each item to identify intense, instinctual responses. It does not measure knowledge or skills. The assumption is that when you know your strengths, you can acquire the knowledge and skills to amplify them. You receive a "Strengths Discovery and Action-Planning Guide" based on your results. For this High D, for example, it came as no surprise that the strength themes were: Achiever, Activator, Command, Futuristic, Significance. The great thing about this test is that you have an action plan to accompany the assessment.

I would recommend any company use both the DISC and the Strengths Finder in order to take maximum advantage of the human potential and talent within the organization. This would create a system based on synergy.

System?

Unless the system is organized synergistically, no amount of testing will lead to improvement. Compare the U.S. Government to the U.S. Military. The Military has a system that works. Strangely, I have never talked with a draftee who didn't believe his military experience was one of the most valuable of his lifetime. True, my conversations have been limited to people who were either educated when they went in or who went on to get "educated" when they got out. They normally have been either high D or high C, and the military, through tests, determined where they could be best utilized – learning languages to do intelligence, developing computer software, overseeing logistics and operations, financial analysis, organizational leadership and management.

Just as manufacturing requires high numbers of High S workers, so also does the military require large numbers of High S for infantry. As "warfare" becomes more and more technology driven, this will be less true. I have had the opportunity for the last ten years to experience military personnel as students in my on-line courses They are intelligent, disciplined, courteous, prompt, dependable, and loyal. We are fortunate to have such fine men and women willing to serve our country.

Do you have a system for organizing your talent and the talent of those around you? Are you building this recognition and assessment of talent into the way you are raising your children? Do you have expectations for your self or for your partner or spouse that are that are unrealistic? That can only lead to frustration and disappointment. When you *replant*, assess your stock of seeds and anticipate your best crop.

Societal and Cultural Implications?

The work of Clare W. Graves and Dr. Don Beck with *Spiral Dynamics*[8] systematizes the organizing codes and principles of the evolution and emergence of human society by an ascending color spiral, from the bottom up: beige – survival and instinct driven, purple – tribal and safety driven, red – egocentric and power driven, blue – authority and order driven, orange – strategic and success driven, green – community and people driven, yellow – systemic and process oriented, turquoise – holistic and synthesis oriented.

The attempts to impose democracy in the Middle East, blue and orange principles upon purple and red codes, have resulted in destabilization and chaos. We now see purple and red, tribal conquest and domination as Isis, tapping into the technological expertise of the orange and threatening the values of the top half of the spiral. The United States invaded Iraq and became a key player in this disruption. "Arab Spring" is chaos.

Where are you in this spiral of human emergence? Does it have implications for your personal endeavors, those of your family, those of your business. If this subject interests you, Said Dawlabani, a macroeconomics expert, takes a whole-systems approach to economic sustainability in *MeMEnomics: the Next-Generation Economic System*[9] I would urge you to regard your life and work as the next generation economic system and to *replant* accordingly.

What we call real estate – the solid ground to build a house on – is the broad foundation on which nearly all the guilt of the world rests. . . . The author has provided himself with a moral - the truth, namely, that the wrong-doing of one generation lives into the successive ones, and divesting itself of every temporary advantage, becomes a pure and uncontrollable mischief; and he would feel it a singular gratification if this romance might effectually convince mankind – or indeed, any one man – of the folly of tumbling down an avalanche of ill-gotten gold, or real estate on the heads of an unfortunate posterity, thereby to main and crush them, until the accumulated mass shall be scattered abroad in its original atoms.

Nathaniel Hawthorne, *The House of Seven Gables*[1]

Now since the prince must make use of the characteristics of beasts he should choose those of the fox and the lion, though the lion cannot defend himself against snares and the fox is helpless against wolves. One must be a fox in avoiding traps and a lion in frightening wolves. Such as choose simply the role of a lion do not rightly understand the matter. Hence a wise leader cannot and should not keep his word when keeping it is not to his advantage or when the reasons that made him give it are no longer valid. If men were good, this would not be a good precept, but since they are wicked and will not keep faith with you, you are not bound to keep faith with them. We must be like the lion and the fox.

Niccolo Machiavelli, *The Prince*[2]

BE A GREAT PIRATE

Commodities discovered and distributed

WHEN HAWTHORNE OBSERVES "all the guilt of the world rests" on real estate, he acknowledges this perfect planet has been carved up and passed out over the centuries by individuals who have wielded their power and manipulation over others, who have played the lion and the fox. R. Buckminster Fuller called these people the Great Pirates, or GP's, and he conceived of the first ones as adventurers with courage and curiosity. They moved from their island of birth by canoe to explore the next island where they discovered commodities unknown at home. This was the origin of trade. At first it might have been as simple as a banana island, a coconut island, a pineapple island, a mango island, and a basket island. The Great Pirate knew where to find each fruit and where to find the basket to hold it.

Beginning of sovereign power

As the Great Pirates accumulated knowledge about the location of different commodities, they also established power for themselves. They were the only ones who knew where everything was. As the task of handling the whole enterprise on their own became too overwhelming, they installed token kings to oversee each distribution center, endowing them with the visual and exterior symbols of power: crown, scepter, robe, and elegant hut. They were the sovereign power, i.e. the reigning power over the territory assigned to them by the Great Pirate.

Kings: control by specialization

Each king knew the functioning of his own island, but knew nothing about the other islands. He did as the GP told him. Each king was instructed to assign specific jobs on the island. The best mathematician was made treasurer, the best memorizer the secretary, the best organizer the manager of operations. No one was to know anyone else's job, only his own. The only other person, other than the king, who could know every job description was the king's son. In that way knowledge, which is power, was localized in the ruling family. Fuller believes this was the "origin of specialization," a method to keep each individual narrow in scope and limited.

Carving up the planet

As the kingdoms of the kings became more powerful, the kings began exploration on their own, or so it appeared. Always, however, they acted with the GP's guidance, knowledge, and supervision. The GP's preferred to work in the background, anonymously calling the shots and controlling the resources. So the kings then marched on continents, on North America, announcing one part to the King of Spain, another part to the King of England. They were represented by people such as Christopher Columbus who didn't know where he was going, and didn't know where he was when he got there. That's why we have Indians in the Americas: the confused chap thought he was in India. The kings marched on Africa, claiming one territory for the King of Belgium, another for the King of the Netherlands, another for the King of England, and so on. Always the envoy of the king planted a flag and claimed sovereign power, that is, ruling power. The indigenous people let them do it, often without a fight. They may have had law- givers in their tribes, but they had no lawyers.

The beginning of real estate

This was the beginning of real estate, the planet-wide determiner of true "wealth" because we can measure it, we can't move it, but we can transfer it once we take title to it. Even the word "title" takes us back to the "sovereign" roots of real estate. The original inhabitants, we call them indigenous, at least in the

United States, believed that Mother Earth belonged to every-one and had neither the concept nor the vocabulary for such a seizure. Thus our planet was carved up and claimed by kings who reigned sovereign over their territory. The history of man at war is the history of man laying claim to real estate, more often than not in the name of Jehovah, or Allah, or God. In the great war, the Second World War, both sides of the European front declared God as their champion. Today we have Isis seizing territory and beheading the infidels in the name of Allah.

Spanish Land Grants

The Spanish explorers came to the Americas: Cortez, Ponce de Leon, Balboa; and everywhere they went, they laid claim for the King of Spain. Is there anything more ridiculous than the historical "facts" we were taught in school, that Ponce de Leon discovered Florida, and Balboa discovered the Pacific Ocean? Southern California was parceled out in Spanish Land Grants from the King of Spain. Real estate empires were formed. The city of Irvine, California, now boasting the highest valued property in Orange County, is built on a Spanish Land Grant said to have been won by a member of the Irvine family in a poker game.

Although the story may be apocryphal, one may well ask how such a story could even be bandied about. Truly, the aggressive, assumptive seizure of property from inhabitants too ignorant and naïve to realize what was happening actually took place. Once they were dispossessed and displaced, they had no power. Father Junipero Serra traveled the coast of California founding missions - San Diego, San Juan Capistrano, Santa Monica, Santa Barbara, San Jose, Santa Cruz, San Francisco, to name only a few. The priests in the missions, we have been told, worked with the indigenous people, teaching them what they knew. When Pope Francis canonized Father Serra, however, the local Indians protested Mission San Juan Capistrano as the location for the ceremony on the grounds that their people were treated cruelly by the Catholic priest.

Indian Reservations

Sites with "worthless" real estate

As we consider the history of the North American Indians, we know that the early pilgrim settlers would have had great difficulty surviving without their help. Yet just as the pilgrims entered a land controlled by a distant king, so also did that king claim control of the indigenous residents. When the newcomers declared independence and wrested power from the king, the new government assumed sovereignty over those who first welcomed them. The Indians were pushed and pulled by the wars of the invaders. In the French and Indian War, most Indians fought with the French against the British; yet the Senecas fought with the British. As the U.S. government expanded into new territories, the Indian lands were seized, and their people were sent off to reservations. The land was carefully selected as the worst real estate in the United States.

Sovereign power exempt from rights of U.S. citizens

Ironically, under that real estate, the tribes have sometimes found natural resources, making them wealthy. The Cherokees, for instance, moved by forced walk on the Trail of Tears to their Oklahoma reservation, became wealthy from the oil under their land. A further irony, the Indians were given sovereign power over their territory, independent from the U.S. government. Although this was designed to deny them the benefits of American citizenship, it means also that their territory is independent from U.S. laws and restrictions.

As the Indians have educated themselves in the ways of power, their own Harvard graduate GP's have emerged; and they have turned this to their advantage, with banks, casinos, and bingos, immune to lawsuits, exempt from most taxes, and excluded from labor laws. Now the government regards this as an "area of concern" because it "wasn't what was meant" when the Indians were first segregated from the rights, privileges, and opportunities of living in America, their original home, but their denied nation.

Great Pirates always in the background

Great Pirates do not run for office, do not expose themselves to the public, do not divulge their *modus operandi*. They work through other people. As the sovereign nations have matured and granted voting rights to their people, elected officials have replaced the kings, but still with the backing and control of the Great Pirates. It has reached ridiculous proportions today when "Super Pacs" attempt to control election outcomes with their contributions. $2.2 billion was spent on the presidential election in 2012. 2016 will exceed that. The fund raising capacity of the candidates determines their ability to control the "climate of opinion" through manipulation of the media. Even Trump finally yielded to accepting donations.

Joseph Kennedy: the curse of the Great Pirate?

Our twentieth century in the United States is absorbed with the story of the Kennedy family: So much charm, so much dedication to public service, so much potential, so much money, yet so much tragedy. After the death in a plane crash of John Kennedy Jr., the only son of John F. Kennedy and Jacqueline Bouvier Kennedy, the media began to talk about a curse on the family, a curse from the ill-got fortune of the father, Joseph Kennedy, a great pirate who acquired his wealth as a rum-runner, trading in liquor during prohibition when it was illegal.

They were asking, was it this origin in evil that led to the chain of tragedy: the early death of the first-born son, Joseph, in World War II; the assassinations of John F. Kennedy when he was President, and of Bobby Kennedy, when he was running for president; the early death of Kathleen; the murky circumstances surrounding the drowning of Ted Kennedy's companion and his flight from the scene of the accident.

A dynasty of "kings"

Curse or no curse, it is an emblematic case of the great pirate and the king, or rather, President, in our American democracy. Although he served one brief appointment as Ambassador to Great Britain, Joseph Kennedy could never have run for office. His fortune was not appropriately acquired, and he would have been too rough-hewn to be elected. He worked as a Great Pirate, gaining social stature and respectability by marrying into the Fitzgerald family, an old Boston family with pedigree. He had twelve children by his wife, Rose.

Of those twelve, three sons rose to high positions in the U.S. government, as senators and then one as president, John Fitzgerald Kennedy. Joseph Kennedy was behind the scenes during his son's campaign for President, directing and controlling the activities and the flow of money, securing the support of the Mob and the labor unions. He was a master at manipulating public opinion. When the book, *Profiles in Courage*, was published, it is said that he bought up all of the copies and warehoused them, thus making his son's book a best seller overnight. Had Joseph Kennedy not suffered a stroke and been incapacitated right after John's election, he would have controlled the conduct of the Presidency and perhaps prevented the events that led to the assassination of his sons, especially Bobby's assault on the mafia and organized labor who helped get his son elected. One does not bite the hand that feeds you.

The hierarchy of having

Other than cynical awareness, what good does it do to look at the history of the world as the manipulation of GPs? It can place in perspective where we feel we are in the "hierarchy of having." If it is true that seven "moneyed" families control the financial world of the planet, then life appears pretty much to be divided: The *haves* and the *have-nots*; the *ins* and the *outs*; the *givers* and the *takers*; the *shapers* and *recipients*; the *powerful* and the *powerless*; the *controllers* and the *controlled*. Those who *have*, who are *in*, who *give*, and who *shape* know abundance, self-confidence, and presumably peace and harmony. Those who *have-not*, who are *out*, who *take* what's handed to them and who *receive* policy, who are *powerless*, live in scarcity, insecurity, and envy.

Kings as executioners

Let us suppose that specialization began when the Great Pirates appointed kings and told them to assign jobs to their constituents, but to not let anyone do or know anyone else's job. If anyone else knew what he and his son knew, then he could be king. In fact, the fascinating thing about being on the high side - *Have, In, Give, Shape, Power, Control* - is that as soon as you're there, you worry about staying there, about protecting what you have and know, about keeping the other side in its place. The word *execute* means to carry out. Yet note how the connotation of *execution* comes first into our minds as an act of violence, of seizing life from another. It also applies to seizing *life work* from another.

The history of the kings of England provides a perfect example. As soon as a man became king, usually by executing the king before him, he was uneasy about staying king, began to execute potential opponents, and ultimately was executed himself by the next king. Probably most of us know Shakespeare's play, *Macbeth*, as well as any. As you may recall from the play, the moment Macbeth has murdered to become king, "Macbeth has murdered sleep." It begins his path of *paranoia*, until both he and Lady Macbeth, overcome by guilt and anxiety, lose their ability to function effectively. They madly begin to destroy any potential contenders to the throne, the competition. Yet, ultimately they are defeated when the "woods come to Dunsinane," the prediction of the three witches. They are attacked by soldiers who march on them with trees tied to their helmets, a veritable moving woods.

Competitive seizure and elimination

You don't have to be king of anything to know the fear of protecting a position once you've got the job. This is what we learn from the Great Pirates: how to seize and how to keep control. There are exceptions. Bill Gates surrounded himself with the brightest and the best at Microsoft because he came from a place of self-confidence and self-satisfaction. The same is true of Howard Schultz, the CEO of Starbucks. As one moves away from the attitude of a Gates or Schultz, at the other end of the spectrum, we have large institutions, especially bureaucratic ones, that operate as formalized GP's, with boxes, boundaries, and rules for each position.

Each working individual exists in a situation somewhere between the two extremes. People in established positions often feel driven to box in and put down others who might either pose as threats or make them look inadequate. Have you ever been told you are not to overstep your bounds? When you are at the bottom in the "hierarchy of having," you belong to the "company store." You have no sovereignty over your destiny. An aggressive, ambitious, bright young person may be labeled "arrogant," and the word may go out: "Watch out for him. He's ambitious."

Self-realization: self-employment

In a bureaucratic institution, a kluge operation, one is the recipient of a system designed by GP's long gone who left in place unquestioned process and procedure. Old rules form the basis of decision-making, and people in power positions use them for self-protection.

If this book has one essential message, it would be that self-realization can best be achieved through an attitude of self-employment. Self-employment exists in thought and is a state of mind. When you hold yourself as the president of your own company, interfacing with clients and colleagues, you retain your integrity, and you retain sovereignty over your activities. You are a great pirate in your life, determining the flow of activity, the course of your path.

The pinnacle and the base

Emerson says, "the pinnacle cannot exceed the base." In my own career in *academia*, which stretched over two decades, the base stood, but the system resisted the pinnacle. I am using myself as an example of one for whom self-realization and self-employment are inextricably linked, something I didn't know until I found myself in the role of an administrator in a bureaucracy. This is a story about hitting a wall and then being challenged to figure out the appropriate environment to use my abilities. Each of us faces this challenge and will not know satisfaction until we have achieved this understanding.

As a "high achiever," I had put myself through all my degrees, finished a doctoral degree, taken a job at a small women's college as an assistant professor, been promoted to chairman of the department, assumed leadership in every one of the major committees in the college, written a few articles published in acceptable journals, taught classes from the beginning to the present in English literature, and developed a following of students and faculty. This is what an academician is supposed to do.

When the financial problems at that small college became so severe that it began to consume my life, and when the leadership of the college fell in a way that made me uncomfortable, I accepted an administrative position at a University directing an academic program in a residence hall. It required that I give up the tenure granted at the end of my third year at my former institution. It didn't occur to me to worry about it since I had been continuously employed since the age of twelve.

Accidental achievement ok

Once again, a pattern of success emerged, easily and effort-lessly, just as Emerson's little bark makes its way to sea. My vision expanded to the creation of another academic program in a second residence hall, based upon the model of Yale's residential colleges and the University of Michigan's residential college. This would give the students a focus for creative living in an energized academic environment. It was the late '70s. The University was a party school. The students were consumed with alcohol and drugs; and in the morning, the halls would be littered with bottles and cans from the partying the night before. In my 8:00 a.m. class in Humanities, my students would sit bleary-eyed through my sales pitch for Aeschylus, Plato, Sophocles, Euripides, and Homer.

Drive and ambition not ok

As my passion to change and improve this situation grew into a plan with specific goals, others followed and supported me. In fact, we moved the second residential program through every necessary committee with record speed, all the way to the Chancellor for final approval. Up to that time, my accomplishments were made with my left hand, putting my family before a career and without taking myself seriously. As my efforts began to reflect greater earnestness and zeal, however, forces simultaneously began to align against me. Drive and ambition are acceptable in entrepreneurs, but not in bureaucrats. It is worse if you are a woman. This was, of course, before Sheryl Sandberg had the audacity to encourage women to *Lean In.*

Lowest common denominator

In my experience, the lowest common denominator ultimately dominates every bureaucratic institution. Whenever an individual even appears to be rocking that lowest common denominator, the power structure rallies to obliterate it. The system does not tolerate innovation. Protection of the *status quo* informs and shapes the process of decision-making. We certainly saw it in action with the 2013 IRS scandal when the woman in charge of the Cincinnati office took the Fifth Amendment. We saw it again in the FBI Director's decision that Hillary Clinton's excessive "carelessness" with classified information was without criminal intent.

The work obsession

Since I had been working so hard all my life, keeping my "nose to the grindstone," the big picture of how the power structure actually functions was never clear to me. On the one hand, in retrospect, the university represented for me the safe haven of the insecure academic. Yet, on the other hand, in my heart I was a self-made entrepreneur, and consequently for *academia*, "a duck out of water."

All my life I knew nothing but work. It was taught in my home. Work, the idea of work, so Puritanical, so Germanic, narrowly defined existence for me. Emerson says, "Do your work and I shall know you." It was not that kind of work, not the *calling*. It was work, the being busy, each mediocre accomplishment a means for a definition of self. I note a difference between "definition of self" and "self esteem."

In the course of this activity, I never had a room of my own. During my childhood, someone was always living with us: aunts, uncles, cousins, my sisters. There was never quite enough room, and my needs and wants were subordinate to circumstances. In fact, in my mind, in accordance with my sentence," subordination was the appropriate state and self-assertion the inappropriate state. This was true with my teachers, my parents, and then my husband. The outer self-assurance, confidence, effectiveness enclosed the inner assumption of unworthiness. When I chose Virginia Woolf, the author of *A Room of One's Own*, as the subject for my doctoral dissertation, it was surely an Emersonian act of "compensation."

The safe haven

Academia was the perfect place for someone with my issues so long as I didn't take myself seriously or question subordination. My complexes remained hidden even to me because I just kept working. When that work became a mission and a form of self-definition, however, when it became really important to me, it was taken away. The head of housing considered me both a nuisance and a threat because he was afraid I would go through the University and put an academic program in every residence hall. He was right; that was my intent. In the meantime, that same Humanities Department, built into this newly created program and showcased as the cornerstone, ganged up against me behind my back to eliminate me and take over what I had created.

Be paranoid

My focus on activity and results and my basic naivety blinded me to the machinations occurring around me. Where was Donald Trump then? Be paranoid! Get even! When I left, they replaced me with three men, and then the Humanities Department moved in and took over. So many power plays over such a piddling pond!

Hassling the hierarchy

This experience highlighted some of the more challenging aspects of my personality, especially impatience and "envisioning zeal." My husband at the time would shrink fearfully away from my tendency to view reality from my imagination, i.e., the way it would be when I had molded it to my vision. His concern was what it would take from him to realize to my envisioned reality. The greater my exuberance, the more he would feel threatened. My operation with the university was similar: going over and around people, not "observing the hierarchy," moving as a bulldozer. That's exactly what an entrepreneur does – the High D

So long as I was in the classroom, the entrepreneurial side manifested in creative ways to present the material to the students. As an initiator rather than a presider, I actually lack the basic constitution to be an administrator. Academic administrators spend their entire days in meetings where little is accomplished. My favorite analogy is taking a male dog for a walk. Each person in a meeting pees on the tree, gets his name in the minutes, and the job is complete. The tree is watered, the day is over, major issues are tabled, and the next meeting is set. It drove me crazy.

Thankful for faults

A part of me is still the person who had this experience, but I am impatient with her now. She irritates me because her egotistic perspective blew the puny little plot of land she was tilling into such importance. The program actually still thrives, after 30 years. Several years after I left, when my son was an undergraduate at Harvard, he directed one of the Harvard Student Agencies and hired a summer school student from the University. The student said, "I'm in this great two-year academic program. It's the best thing the University has." My son said, "Yes, I know about that program. My mother created it." Institutions, says Emerson, are the "lengthened shadow" of the individual. The individual is long gone, and the institution assumes a vitality of its own.

Worthy of compassion

This woman, the one who makes me impatient, also has my compassion. I was shattered for three reasons: 1) I defined myself by work, and my work was taken away. 2) I prided myself on successful achievement, and I was punished for success. 3) I assumed that all of my life I would work for someone else, and that if I played the game properly, I would have a solid career. My identity belonged to the structure, to the system, to the hierarchy, rather than to myself. My life was outer directed and determined, not inner directed and determined. To be punished for success turned everything I had worked for upside down. I was disoriented.

Inevitable calamity

This was the beginning of a path of life from the inside out rather than from the outside in. It was one of those moments defined by Emerson when I was forced to shed the house I had outgrown, and it required a calamity to jolt me on to the next step. Certainly, I would do many things differently now. Today the obstacles would present themselves as challenges placed in my path for a purpose. Since my life path has led me into mediation training, there would be more listening and less talking. Emerson's observation that "every man in his lifetime needs to thank his faults" sums up this experience. Being who I was at the time, brought about a turn in the road that led me down a far different path, one probably more suited to my temperament and certainly more tolerant of change and zeal.

New navigation tools

I was forced to become a "great pirate." I was forced to *reset*, *reboot*, and *replant*. My departure from *academia* led me to develop aspects of myself I didn't know existed. Because the University of Michigan believed that philosophy and mathematics were co-equivalent in perfecting logical thinking, I avoided math. Similarly, I backed away from economics because it was reputed to be too hard and a bad grade might jeopardize my scholarships. For myriad wrong reasons, I shunned a way of thinking and an approach to interpreting reality for which I had a definite aptitude.

The first major new direction in my life, training as a stock-broker, made me a salmon swimming up-stream. My class was full of people who were MBA's in finance, real estate brokers, CPA's. From the shelter of the university, I didn't have a clue how the real world worked. Yet with all of this apparent limitation, I had within me the ability to master this new field, to pass the Series 7, and then later to master financial analysis of commercial real estate for acquisition.

A matter of zeroes

The sales training as a stock broker centered on cold calling. They started us out qualifying buyers for municipal bonds. We had a list of people to call, and our first statement would be, "This requires a minimum investment of $5000. Would that be a problem for you?" I literally choked over that statement for at least the first fifty calls. As an academic I had never dreamed about spending that much money on something to put away in a safe deposit box. Over the course of my career I have come to realize it is just a matter of more zeroes to go from $5,000 to $50,000,000. The people are pretty much the same. It is just a different product.

More zeroes, same quirks

Once I became accustomed to zeroes, I got carried away by them for a while. During the frantic period when the Japanese were buying out American commercial real estate, I participated in a team that put an office complex for $250,000,000 into escrow. The deal didn't close because the buyers at the end were not able to come up with the funds, but the adrenalin rush was great. I also wore myself out for several years trying to sell 1100 acres of raw land in Malibu with ocean frontage. The owner, who once had owned two miles along the coast of the Pacific Ocean, wanted $80,000,000 cash, a big chunk for a property not permitted by the Coastal Commission. He loved to show the property to buyers, to buy them a lobster and clam chowder lunch at his favorite restaurant, to make it a glorious day-outing, but I finally realized he didn't want to let go of the property. On weekends he would take his little lawn chair out to the property and just sit there.

Although I brought him several capable buyers, he never would accept their offers. I finally gave up when I took him an offer for $20,000,000 cash and $564,000 a month for the next twenty years. He made a classic comment: "Adrian, you know I can't live on $564,000 a month." The other broker called me the next day and said, "I don't understand how he can smile while he is making such obnoxious statements." I explained that he was on his third face lift, and the last one left him with a constant stretched smile.

Just like you and me

In business and in life today, I carry as a touchstone a conversation that I once had with Ann Love, the wife of Governor John Love of Colorado. As a young assistant professor, only twenty-seven, I was the faculty's elected representative to a search committee for a new president of the college. The committee was chaired by Walt Kobel, the developer of Vail, Colorado, and the members of the committee were well-recognized state leaders, to me absolutely awesome. The candidates who came for interviews were equally eminent, and I was impressed by the way Ann Love always put them at their ease, always knew exactly what to say and when to say it. When I finally knew her well enough to ask her about it, she said, "I just remember that they are just like you and me. They get hungry; they have to go the bathroom; they need to call home to their families." As the zeroes in the numbers have increased in the products I deal with, I remember her words. The consumers, the people buying, are just like you and me. The sellers have the same anxieties, neuroses, and quirks.

Mastery

Each time I have changed career, I have mastered a new vocabulary. That is the bottom line. The infinitive "to master" is critical. That is what the Great Pirates did, and that is what they continue to do. They create sovereignty, control, through mastery. The Great Pirate techniques stood me in good stead: read for comprehension, master the new vocabulary, discern the crucial from the tangential, predict what would be stressed as essential knowledge to pass the examination.

That is the method to master a new specialization. Now that I have done it several times, each time it gets easier, perhaps because having done it once, the assurance is there to do it again. The adrenalin charge of the challenge has replaced the anxiety. Both are stimulants to the body, but one moves you forward, and the other stops you in your tracks. Charge up and move forward.

Transfer of skills

Further, all of the skills as a teacher, a counselor, and an administrator have been essential in each undertaking. Because both financial services and real estate understanding came to me as an adult learner, I can intuitively uncover areas of confusion in my clients and can clarify issues simply and directly. With a contract, I often teach the contract as I write it, so nothing is left unstated or obfuscated. Further, since most decisions we make in life initiate first from emotion and second by reason, my intuitive powers and my listening skills are more important than any amount of book learning.

Out of control

The issue of control, of keeping someone "in his place" because he may be a threat, is very common in the workplace. My example is an extreme because *academia* is so bureaucratized and the players are so boxed in by the system. Yet, similar situations arise in any institution. Steve Jobs was fired by the company he created. And then they had to hire him back.

If you're too good at what you do, your boss is afraid you will get her job. If you have total enthusiasm for your work, and you find yourself among others who have grown stale and dreary, the light of your star will be drenched lest it illuminate the dullness evoked by your competitors. Do not believe that you are a victim of these circumstances. Rather, know and accept that you have been challenged by them so that you may discover within yourself the resources for greater growth. Let go of the piano top. Let your light shine, if not where you are, then somewhere else. It will be better for you and better for everyone else. Be out of control.

Beyond definition

In his book, *The End of Work*,[3] Jeremy Rifkin predicted that by approximately 2020 there will be no blue collar jobs in the manufacturing sector and that even the majority of our service jobs will be replaced by automation. In the July/August 2016 issue of *INC*, Amy Webb lists many of the go-between jobs that will disappear momentarily – creating opportunities for automation entrepreneurs.[3] A protest against World Trade will not stop the momentum. Yet the truth of technology is that it changes so fast, one's "specialty" is constantly in jeopardy of being eliminated. Check Amy's list to see if you are one of them. We need to know that we can master any new field, that we are not limited by external forces. Nothing exists in the universe except thought and energy. When you think of yourself as self-employed, as the Great Pirate, it changes your orientation toward your employment. Be an independent contractor in your mind.

Knowledge the key

Knowledge is the key to moving from the vulnerable low side-- *Have-Nots, Outsiders, Takers, Recipients, Powerless, Controlled*-- to the high side--*Haves, Ins, Givers, Shapers, Empowered, In Control.* It is increasingly impossible today for those who have knowledge to keep it to themselves because we have access from so many sources opened by the computer and the Internet. We all have the ability to learn everyone else's job, i.e. to move out of the specialization that keeps us in a narrow niche, vulnerable to downsizing and elimination. If we master the tools of comprehensive thinking, we can master any field at any time.

No limits

We are not limited by birth or station from access to knowledge. We can become educated at home, at community colleges, by distance learning. We have no set timetable. Education and learning are life-long. We do not need stockbrokers to become investors. We can trade over the Internet. The commodity market isn't just for Great Pirates

Your tools

The tools and concepts presented here will prove useful in gaining confidence, in thinking comprehensively, and in establishing sovereignty over your life. The purpose of this book is to help you get your mind-set on the high side, to assist you in your move from scarcity to abundance, from vulnerability to empowerment. As we realize that we can now all be Great Pirates within our realm, the control of others diminishes, loses its dominance. You can get off the hamster wheel. You can *reset*, *reboot* and *replant*.

Blessed past

As Emerson points out to us in his essay "Compensation," adversity forces us to leave behind old associations, old patterns of behavior, old ways of approaching problems. It brings out our resilience, our survival instinct; and it taps abilities we never knew we had. We leave behind the house we have outgrown:

> A fever, a mutilation, a cruel disappointment, a loss of wealth, a loss of friends, seems at the moment unpaid loss, and unpayable. But, the sure years reveal the deep remedial force that underlies all facts. The death of a dear friend, wife, brother, lover, which seemed nothing but privation, somewhat later assumes the aspect of a guide or genius; for it commonly operates revolutions in our way of life, terminates an epoch of infancy or of youth which was waiting to be closed, breaks up a wonted occupation, or a household, or style of living, and allows the formation of new ones more friendly to the growth of character.[4]

CONCLUSION

As you redefine yourself as the Great Pirate in control of your destiny, you are no longer chained to the wheel. You are the sower of the seed. You emerge from the dark of the moon into the light.

You have pushed the *reset* button by acknowledging there are no mistakes, only opportunities to discover the truth. You know yesterday's adversity created a space in your life where you can safely let go of the piano tops because you no longer need them.

You have *rebooted* by envisioning your big picture and anticipating your problem solving ability and comprehensive thinking. Your true wealth will take you wherever you have committed to go.

You have *replant*ed by building leverage and synergy into your undertakings and by envisioning yourself as a Great Pirate.

When Fuller wrote *Operating Manual for Spaceship Earth* in 1969, he compared humanity to a tiny chick just at the point where it's ready to break through the shell, when the nutriment is almost gone and the chick is ready to move with its own legs and wings:

> My own picture of humanity today finds us just about to step out from amongst the pieces of our just one-second-ago broken eggshell. Our innocent, trial-and-error-sustaining nutriment is exhausted. We are faced with an entirely new relationship to the universe. We are going to have to spread our wings of intellect and fly or perish; that is, we must dare immediately to fly by the generalized principles governing universe and not by the ground rules of yesterday's superstitious and erroneously conditioned reflexes. And as we attempt competent thinking, we immediately begin to reemploy our innate drive for comprehensive understanding. [1]

Free: thoughts, ideas, promises

Certainly we have broken through that shell, and we have begun to fly by the generalized principles of leverage, synergy, and true wealth at exponential rates. The distribution is still uneven. We have those who "got it" and those who still are "getting it." The obstacles, however, that used to hold us back aren't there anymore. We all have access to the same tools as Jack Ma, Mark Zuckerberg, Tim Cook, Larry Price. True wealth is abundant, growing exponentially, and free. Thoughts are free, ideas are free, promises are free. We can all use *Expectation*, *Belief*, and *Word*, all free, at any second of any minute of any hour to create exactly what we want. The personal employment of competent thinking and comprehensive understanding will expand for each of us as we enlarge our personal big picture. Prosperity must follow as the night follows the day.

There are many books and magazines now that chart the uprising of the entrepreneur, the great pirates of our day. We have more than 27 million entrepreneurs in the United States, and $128 billion in global venture capital money was raised in 2015.

To change your thinking, jump in and read. It will help you create your big picture. Sean Ammirati, an instructor at Carnegie Mellon University, who sold his company to LinkedIn, charts the success of ten of them in *The Science of Growth: How Facebook Beat Friendster – and How Nine Other Startups Left the Rest in the Dust*.[2] The magazines *Inc* and *Fast Company* focus on entrepreneurs. The *Forbes Magazine* accounts of billionaires tell how they did it. In case you haven't noticed, all of these books and magazines are available on-line from your local library.

If you are out of work, network, join linked-in. Sign up, suit up, show up and speak up. Don't fool yourself that sending out a resume is looking for a job. It doesn't work that way anymore. Assess your strengths and develop them. Write them down and read them every day. Say, "yes." You never know where it will take you, but you know that "no" will take you nowhere.

Be fooled out of your limits

We are the only creature who can be whatever we choose to be, can select our incarnation. We can think it, and we can be it, like Emerson's young man from New Hampshire, a cat landing on its feet, tiller of the earth, poet, statesman, astronaut, frogman, painter, sculptor. Elon Musk has pre-sold millions of

TESLAs before they even begin production, sends out rockets and expects to visit Mars. Man has "visions that fool him out of his limits."[3] The poet Robinson Jeffers declares: "Humanity is the mold to break away from, the crust to break through, the coal to break into fire, the atom to be split."[4]

APPENDIX

Exercise Questions for *Get Off the Hamster Wheel*

The questions are organized by Chapter. You may choose to just read the questions and think about your answers. For most significant results, write down the questions and write out your answers. At the end of each set, summarize what you have discovered about yourself from doing the exercise. Please note the questions are open, often anticipating you will finish the sentence.

THE SENTENCE

I never thought of myself as being "sentenced." Yet, as I review the attitudes and beliefs I have had about myself, I observe my parents and family had specific expectations about my future. Here are some of the things they said and did that influenced me.

My mother:

My father:

My siblings:

My grandparents:

In school, my earliest memories of my classmates' attitudes toward me are:

As I progressed through school, I reinforced my "public image" by this behavior:

MAKING ENDS MEET

The areas in my life where I presently feel most stress are:

Job:

Money:

Family obligations

Relationship with significant other:

Children:

Quality time:

Parents:

I nurture myself by:

My greatest fear is:

When I feel afraid, I deal with my fear by:

INHERITED BELIEFS

I never thought about things like race consciousness or

climate of opinion, yet when I think about it, here are some of the ideas I just took for granted:

People who were poorer than I were:

People who were richer than I were:

People who were dumber than I were:

People who were smarter than I were:

People who had different colored skin were:

People who didn't talk as I talked were:

There were certain people I was not supposed to talk to because:

I did or didn't go to church because:

I thought if I did something bad, I would be punished by:

I thought God looked like:

I thought the devil looked like:

WHOSE IDEA AM I?

My earliest childhood dreams for myself came from many places: stories, movies, comic books, radio and television shows. As I remember those dreams, they were:

When I played games with other children, like school, or theater, or doctor, the part I wanted to play was:

When people asked me what I wanted to be when I grew up, I said:

This is what I really was thinking when they asked that question:

I knew when my parents asked that question, this is the answer they expected:

When I disappointed my parents, I felt:

When I lied to please my parents, I felt:

I still remember when I couldn't do what my first boy/girlfriend wanted me to do:

The first time I really felt disappointed with myself that I can remember is:

EASY DOES IT

Emerson meant to instruct and to inspire us with the analogy of the boat sailing so easily, without obstruction. He believes when we are doing the right work, following the right vocation, motivated by purpose and intention, the path opens effortlessly before us.

My mind may accept this inspiration, but it encounters disbelief in my heart because:

The thing I enjoyed doing most when I was a child was:

The contests I remember winning were:

I hated people who were good at things I couldn't do because:

The thing people have praised me most for is:

When I got praised for my achievement, I would say:

I always thought the things I could do most easily had little value because:

It's hard for me to remember things I did right, but I remember screwing up these things:

When things are hard for me, then I feel:

I always thought I couldn't make my living by what comes most easily to me because:

NO MISTAKES: Only Opportunities to Discover the Truth

Fuller notes: "One of humanity's prime drives is to understand and be understood. All other living creatures are designed for highly specialized tasks. Man seems unique as the comprehensive comprehender and coordinator of local universe affairs." Man comprehends through trial and error. Thus, we conclude: "There are no mistakes, only opportunities to discover the truth."

This exercise is designed to assist you in re-framing your mistakes so that you begin to see them as opportunities. From each one you will be able to see that "you can't learn less" and your know-how can only increase.

Did you grow up thinking it was bad to make mistakes?

How were you punished for mistakes?

What do you say to yourself when you make a mistake?

INVENTORY OF MISTAKES

1. Past Week

List the worst mistakes you made over the past week:

What did you learn from each one?

Generalization: How did your know-how increase?

   2. Past Month

List the worst mistakes you made over the past month:

What did you learn from each one?

Generalization: How did your know-how increase?

   3. Past Year

List the worst mistakes you made over the past year:

What did you learn from each one?

Generalization: How did your know-how increase?

   4. Lifetime

List the worst mistakes you made over your lifetime:

What did you learn from each one?

Generalization: How did your know-how increase?

I could reframe my perception of mistakes and begin to see them as opportunities with:

My language, i.e. choice of words, for instance:

My thinking, i.e. choice of thoughts, for instance:

My body language, i.e. open rather than closed, for instance:

PIANO TOPS

List below the "piano tops" you have clung to in your lifetime, temporary lifesavers that you may have made permanent. Next to the piano top, write down the reason you made that choice.

PIANO TOPREASON FOR CHOICE

RELATIONSHIPS:

JOBS:

THINGS

LIFESTYLE CHOICES:

Physical

Intellectual

Spiritual

Are there patterns that you observe: similar attractions, similar anxieties, similar avoidance?

BIG PICTURE and NAVIGATION PATH

Fuller queries: "If it is true that the bigger the thinking becomes the more lastingly effective it is, we must ask: How big can we think.?" He cautions, "...if we don't really know how big is, we may not start big enough."

How big can you think? Since the only restrictions placed upon your big picture are your imagination and belief, what happens if you remove caution and limits?

State your "Big Picture" in words. Be sure to use your name.

My **Big Picture** for my life is:

When my **Big Picture** is achieved:

I will be doing:

I will be living:

I will be wearing:

My circle of five close friends will include:

My sphere of influence will be:

When I look into the mirror, I will feel:

Draw a picture of how you will look when you have achieved your Big Picture. Think of this as a cartoon someone might do of you when you are important enough to be noticed. A caricature always stresses the strongest and most salient features.

Navigation Path

To set my navigation path, here are seven things I need to accomplish, listed in order of priority. For each achievement, I have a measurable goal with a specific timeframe; and I employ leverage and synergy. Seven is the number of completion.

1:

Goal/Timeframe/Leverage/Synergy

2:

Goal/Timeframe/Leverage/Synergy

3:

Goal/Timeframe/Leverage/Synergy

4:

Goal/Timeframe/Leverage/Synergy

5:

Goal/Timeframe/Leverage/Synergy

6:

Goal/Timeframe/Leverage/Synergy

7:

Goal/Timeframe/Leverage/Synergy

WEALTH

Fuller defines "true wealth" when he tells us that "wealth is the product of the progressive mastery of matter by mind" and that "know-how can only increase." We cannot learn less.

In the light of this definition, I know I am wealthy because I have tapped into my know-how by solving the following problems.

At home:

At work:

In my personal relationships:

In my community:

Among my friends:

Fuller states: "Every time man makes a new experiment he always learns more. He cannot learn less. He may learn that what he thought was true was not true." Can you think of three instances when you have "learned more?"

1.

2.

3.

I have always considered wealth material possessions because:

My parents believed wealth is:

In my community the wealthiest and most influential people were:

When I go to the movies and watch television, wealthy people are portrayed as:

My teachers encouraged me to:

I had these thoughts today expressing "Scarcity" or "Fear" that I don't have enough:

The thoughts I had today expressing a feeling of abundance are:

All it would take to know I have enough would be:

I can use my true wealth, my "know-how," along with my understanding of leverage, to create abundance in my life by:

Knowing that I am truly wealthy makes me feel:

LEVERAGE

Fuller asserts: "Once man comprehended that any tree would serve as a lever his intellectual advantages accelerated. Man freed of special-case superstition by intellect has had his survival potentials multiplied millions fold."

We live in a culture that has maximized the concept of leverage metaphysically, giving us ever-increased opportunity to "do more with less." Examine below the extent that you have capitalized upon leverage in your activities.

Places in my life where I use leverage now:

Leverage tools I take for granted, such as the computer and washing machine, are:

Tasks I presently perform where I could benefit from "doing more with less" are:

Leverage could affect my leisure activities if I used it effectively, for instance in making arrangements for:

Travel:

Entertainment:

Physical Fitness:

I could use leverage to increase my productivity at home, in my family, in my church, in my community, by restructuring and creating new systems:

Home:

Family:

Church:

Community:

I could use leverage to increase my productivity at work by:

Hiring an Assistant:

Creating a mailing or using social media:

Duplicating and marketing a creative product or activity:

I can make myself more consciously aware of opportunities to implement leverage in my activities by:

If I increased my productivity by 50%, I would feel:

If I implement leverage effectively in my life, I will decrease stress by:

When I implement leverage effectively in my life, my wealth will increase because:

SYNERGY

Fuller defines synergy as the "behavior of whole systems unpredicted by the separately observed behaviors of any of the system's separate parts or any subassembly of the system's parts." My basic personality determines my behavior within any organizational structure and within any personal relationship.

Based on my understanding of the DISC model, I observe that I am predominately:

Personality:

Type:

Because:

My current work allows me to be myself because:

My current work restricts my self-expression because:

Taking what I have learned about synergy into account, the operation of my workplace could be improved if:

My own productivity could be improved with these synergistic changes in my working environment:

The aspects of synergy I observe functioning effectively in my personal relationships are:

The aspects of synergy I observe not functioning effectively in my personal relationships are:

Problems that could be addressed by taking synergy into account are:

If we were to organize our workplace using the DISC model to assign roles, the people and roles would be organized:

    D

    I

    S

    C

If we were to organize our home using the DISC model to assign roles, the people and roles would be organized:

D

I

S

C

GREAT PIRATE

We often think we are locked into our occupations and professions. This gives us a sense of futility to even contemplate change. We feel that we are "outer" driven, that someone else is in charge of our present and future. When we begin to regard ourselves as the "Great Pirate," we become "inner" driven and know that we can master new fields by acquiring additional skills and knowledge and by learning a new vocabulary. We often believe we have nowhere to go because we have a false perception of where we have been. Take some time to assess a lifetime.

LIFETIME OCCUPATIONS:

List the worst job experiences you have ever had.

Job:

I was expected to do:

The people most closely involved with me were:

When I went to work every day, I felt:

The worst pain I experienced was:

The basic conflict that caused the pain was:

Looking back, I learned this about myself from the pain and conflict:

Job:

I was expected to do:

The people most closely involved with me were:

When I went to work every day, I felt:

The worst pain I experienced was:

The basic conflict that caused the pain was:

Looking back, I learned this about myself from the pain and conflict:

Fuller believes that "society operates on the theory that specialization is the key to success, not realizing that specialization precludes comprehensive thinking." For each occupation listed above, state the specialized skill it required and the comprehensive knowledge you acquired in achieving that specialized skill. Comprehensive knowledge may include such things as following a procedure, mastering a vocabulary, establishing a timetable for completing tasks or fulfilling a discipline, for instance making 20 phone calls a day, etc.

JOB/SPECIALIZED SKILL/COMPREHENSIVE KNOWLEDGE

The areas in my life where I can be in control by accessing my comprehensive knowledge are:

The thought of being in control, of taking control, makes me feel:

In the past, I have preferred to be controlled by others in these situations because:

I can become a Great Pirate if I perceive myself as:

These experiences of a lifetime I have reviewed serve my highest and best good because:

ACKNOWLEDGEMENTS

The literary touchstones, "prologue" to most chapters in this book, are gifts inspired by my teachers at the University of Michigan: Prof. Austin Warren for my introduction to Emerson, Dickinson, Hawthorne and the metaphysical poets; Professor Bennett Weaver for his moving interpretations of Browning, Dante, the Romantic Poets, and the Bible; Professor Gerald Else for his heroic presentation of the Classics; William Frankena for his voyages to Plato's realm of Ideas; Professor G. B. Harrison for his explication and vigorous reading of Shakespeare; Professor James Gindin for his introduction to modern British fiction, especially Woolf and Lawrence; and Professor Herbert Barrows for piloting me through theses on first James Joyce and then Virginia Woolf. The late R. Buckminster injected me with his faith in the future of humanity and made me aware we are sailing on a magnificently designed spaceship whose operation we continually discover. My hundreds of students have challenged me to expand my knowledge, achieve clarity and master technology.

My community service has actually contributed to this undertaking. For nine and a half years, I had the privilege to serve as the Program Director of the Inside Edge Foundation for Education, booking a speaker every Wednesday morning at the University Club of the University of California, Irvine. The 475 writers, scientists, leaders and thinkers heightened my awareness, sharpened my mind and kept me on the cutting edge of innovation. I am grateful for the neurons and dendrites they activated.

I serve on two Boards of Directors that are important to me: The University of Michigan Alumni Association of Orange County (UMAOC) and the Newport Beach Public Library Foundation. Mike Rubin, UM and Michigan Law, hosts the meetings of our Michigan Professionals Business Network that I chair at his Law Office, Rutan and Tucker. Mike always makes me believe what I say is important. To be heard is the greatest gift one can give.

With the Library, I have come full circle. My first "real" job was at the Adrian City Library as a Page for $.50 an hour, shelving books. I spent so much time at the beautiful Carnegie Library that they hired me when I was 12. I do, indeed, know the Dewey Decimal system. The former School of Library Science at the University of Michigan is now called the School of Information. How significant! In Newport Beach we are at the cutting edge of that transition to "information" and the Foundation contributes significantly each year to the library's embrace of technology.

Certain friends and my extended family have been steadfastly by my side. Rev. Patricia Truman offered nudging support and the "divine elbow" with her *What*, *When* and *Why not* queries. In writing and rewriting, I heard the voice of Gail

Minogue, pre-eminent social/economic analyst, urging, "Be heard." Dr. Basia Christ, editor of *Radiance*, published my article "The New Moon," spurring me on with this book. I offer grateful thanks to Debbie O'Byrne for the cover of this book. She graciously accepted the ideas and input of those who contributed to the final product: The brilliant and gifted Karla Guyer designed the wheels within the wheels. The Allard family: Dr. Teresa Allard and Dr. John Allard served as critics, and Jesse Allard provided web design with great patience and attention to detail. Shawn Knapp offered computer crisis management and technical assistance.

Finally, there are those closest to me. I thank my children. My daughter, Kerren Bergman, read my manuscript with fastidious detail, offered painstaking criticism and total loving support. She is always by my side. My son, Charles Proudfit, brought to bear the clear, white light of intellectual challenge and the pragmatic estimation of a man of business. I am always inspired by his commitment to walk his talk "At Work on Purpose."

My parents, LeRoy and Delores Wood, and my grandparents, Cecelia and Columbach Happel and Flora May Wood have living presence in my writing. They taught me to how to plant and how to work, both lifetime gifts that determined my direction and practice.

To Ronald Knapp, my partner in life, I offer thanks for his humor, his constant encouragement and support, his patience with the long hours I spent at the computer, and his exercise of the bragging rights I long ago relinquished to him.

REFERENCE NOTES

Introduction

1. Ralph Waldo Emerson, *Selected Writings of Emerson*, ed. Donald McQuade (NewYork: The Modern Library, 1981), p. 267. All references to Emerson are from this edition and the notes hereafter will indicate them by *Emerson* and the page number.

2. R. Buckminster Fuller, *Operating Manual for Spaceship Earth* (New York: E. P. Dutton, 1963). All references are from this edition and the notes hereafter will indicate them by *Manual* and the page number.

3. *Emerson*, p. 348.

4. Ernest Holmes, *The Science of Mind* (New York: G.P. Putnam's Sons, 1988), p.348.

Part 1. Life's Sentence

The Sentence

1. *Emerson*, p.183.

2. Franz Kafka, "The Judgment," *Psychological Fiction*, ed. Morris Beja (Glenview, Illinois: Scott, Foresman & Company, 1971).

3. Franz Kafka, "The Metamorphosis," *Classics of Modern Fiction: Ten Short Novels*, ed. Irving Howe (New York: Harcourt Brace Jovanovich, Inc., 1980).

Making Ends Meet

1. *Emerson*, p. 145.

2. *Manual*, pp. 37-44.

3. David Friedman, "The Fate of a Nation," *LA Times*, Sunday, August 20, 1995, "Opinion," 1.

4. Marla Dickinson, "The Six O'Clock Scramble," *LA Times*, August 1, 1999, A3.

5. Mary McNamara, "Our Culture of Efficiency Has Made Life Harder," *LA Times*, September 6, 1999, E1.

6. Eric Morath, "Soaring Child-Care Costs Squeeze Families," *The Wall Street Journal*, July 2-3, 2016 A3

7. Robert Kiyosaki, with Sharon L. Lechter, *Rich Dad Poor Dad* (Paradise Valley, Arizona: TechPress, Inc., 1998.

Inherent Evil

1. *Emerson*, p. 183.

2. *Emerson*, p. 160.

3. Nathaniel Hawthorne, *Tales and Sketches* (New York: The Viking Press, 1972), p. 383.

4. Ibid., p. 383-84.

5. Ibid., p. 283-84.

6. Ibid., p. 286-87.

Limits: Living Someone Else's Dream

1. *Emerson*, p. 182.
2. James Joyce, "Araby," *Dubliners* (New York: The Viking Press, 1958) pp. 29-35.
All quotations from this text.

Too Easy: The Oxen and the Eagle

1. *Emerson*, p. 179.
2. Robert Frost, "Fire and Ice," *The Poems of Robert Frost* (New York: The Modern
Library, 1930), p. 232.

Part 2: A Conceptual Framework

We are all Astronauts

1. Miguel de Cervantes Saavedra, *Don Quixote*, trans. Samuel Putnam (New York: The Viking Press, 1949), p. 64.

2. *Manual*, p. 49-50.

3. Carl Sagan, *Cosmos* (New York: Random House, 1980), p. 67.

Trial and Error

1. Emily Dickinson, "'Tis So Much Joy," *Selected Poems of Emily Dickinson* (New York: Random House, 1924), p.4.

2. Emerson, p. 263.

3. Sagan, p. 51-52.

4. Ibid., p. 56.

5. Ibid., p. 64.

6. Ibid., p. 64

7. Ibid., p. 64.

8. Ibid., p. 67.

9. Ibid., p. 142.

10. Christophe Galfard, *The Universe in Your Hand: A Journey through Space, Time, and Beyond* (New York: Flatiron Books, 2016)

11. Carlo Rovelli, *Seven Brief Lessons on Physics* (New York: Riverhead Books, 2016), p. 18.

12. Ibid. p, 19.

The Metaphysical Context

1. *Emerson*, p. 331.

2. *Emerson*, p. 181.

Part 3. Reset

No Mistakes

1. Dante Alleghieri, *Dante's Inferno*, trans. Mark Musa (Bloomington Indiana University Press, 1971), Canto I, l. 1-9.

2. *Emerson*, p. 141.

3. Sophocles, *Oedipus the King*, trans. David Grene, *An Anthology of Greek Drama*, ed. C.A. Robinson, Jr. (New York: Holt, Rinehart and Winston, 1960), p. 53.

4. Ibid., p. 64.

5. *Manual*, p. 92-93.

Piano Tops

1. *Emerson*, p. 171.

2. *Manual*, p. 9.

3. *Emerson*, p. 168.

4. *Manual*, p. 121.

5. Napoleon Hill, *Think and Grow Rich* (New York: Fawcett Books, 1960), p. 221.

Part 4: Reboot

Big Picture

1. Joseph Campbell, *Myths to Live By* (New York: The Viking Press, 1972), p. 259-60.

2. *Emerson*, p. 353.

3. Virginia Woolf, *To the Lighthouse*, (New York: Harcourt, Brace & World, Inc., 1927), p. 9.

4. Ibid., p. 10.

5. Ibid., p. 10-11.

6. Ibid., p. 77.

7. Ibid., p. 88.

8. Ibid., p. 301.

9. Ibid.

10. Ibid., p. 310.

11. *Manual*, p. 59.

12. Ibid., p. 60.

13. Ibid., p. 67.

True Wealth

1. George S. Clason, *The Richest Man in Babylon* (New York: Penguin Books, 1955), p. 152.

2. *Emerson*, p. 698.

3. Ibid., p. 697.

4. *Manual*, p. 83-84.

5. Ibid., p. 85.

6. Ibid., p. 89.

7. *The Edge*, Twentieth Century Fox, 1997, starring Anthony Hopkins and Alec Baldwin.

8. Emerson, p. 485-486.

9. Bill Gates, *The Road Ahead* (New York: Penguin Books, 1993), p. 5.

10. Ibid., p. 34-36.

11. *Manual*, p. 102.

12. Ibid., p 110.

13. Ibid., p. 111.

Part 5 Replant

Leverage: More with Less

1. *Emerson*, p. 479

2. Maynard Keynes, "The General Theory of Employment," *Quarterly Journal of Economics*, Feb. 1937, reprinted in S. E. Harris, ed. *The New Economics*, p. 187. Reprinted in Axel Leijonhufvud, *On Keynesian Economics and the Economics of Keynes: A Study in Monetary Theory* (London: Oxford University Press, 1968), p. 163.

3. Ibid.

4. Ibid, p. 46, reprinted in Leijonhufvud, p. 278.

Synergy

1. *Emerson*, p.332-33.

2. *Emerson*, p.146.

3. Herman Melville, "Bartelby the Scrivener A Story of Wall Street," *Psychological Fiction*, ed. Morris Beja (Glenville, Illinois: Scott, Foresman & Company, 1971, p.235.

4. Rana Foroohar, *Makers and Takers: The Rise of Finance and the Fall of American Business.* (New York: Crown Business Books, 2016)

5. The test with the DISC classification in the results is the Personal Profile System trademarked by Carlson Learning in Minneapolis, Minnesota. To order the test or to get more information about it, call 800 777 9897.

6. Here are some web sites that offer various psychological tests to determine whether your career is right for you: keirsey. com, ansir.com, od-online.com, queendom.com, review. com/birkman/ tms.com.au/questionnaire.html.com, universityoflife.com, test.com.

7. Tom Rath, *Strengths Finder 2.0* (New York: Gallup Press, 2007)

8. Don Beck and Christopher Cowan, *Spiral Dynamics: Mastering Values, Leadership, and Change.* (New York: Wiley/Blackwell, 1996.2005)

9. Said Elias Dawlabani, *MEMEnomics: The Next Generation Economic System* (New York: SelectBooks, Inc. 2013

The Great Pirates

1. Nathaniel Hawthorne, *The House of the Seven Gables* (Cutchogue, New York: Buccaneer Books, 1987), p. viii.

2. Niccolo Machiavelli, *The Prince*, trans. T. G. Bergin (New York: Appleton- Century, Crofts, 1947), p. 51.

3. Jeremy Rifkin, *The End of Work* (New York: G. B. Putnam's Sons, 1995).

4. Amy Webb, "The Industrial Evolution: Get Ready to See These Go-Between Jobs Automated Out of Existence, *INC*, July/August, 2016, p. 84

5. *Emerson*, p. 172.

Conclusion

1. *Manual*, p. 58-59.

2. Sean Ammirati, *The Science of Growth: How Facebook Beat Friendster – and How Nine Other Startups Left the Rest in the Dust* (New York: St. Martin's Press, 2016)

3. Erwin Schrodinger, *My View of the World*, (Cambridge, Cambridge University Press, 1964), p. 95.

4. Robinson Jeffers, *Roan Stallion, Tamar, and Other Poems* (New York: Horace Liveright, 1925), p. 249.

BIBLIOGRAPHY

Sean Ammirati, *The Science of Growth*: *How Facebook Beat Friendster – and How Nine Other Startups Left the Rest in the Dust* (New York: St. Martin's Press, 2016)

Don Beck and Christopher Cowan, *Spiral Dynamics: Mastering Values, Leadership, and Change.* (New York: Wiley/Blackwell, 1996.2005)

Robert Browning, *Poems of Robert Browning*, ed. Donald Smalley: A Riverside Edition (Boston: Houghton Mifflin Co., 1956)

Joseph Campbell, *Myths to Live By* (New York: The Viking Press, 1972)

Joseph Campbell, *The Power of Myth with Bill Moyers*, ed. Betty Sue Flowers (New York: Doubleday 1988)

Miguel de Cervantes Saavedra, *Don Quixote*, trans. Samuel Putnam (New York: The Viking Press, 1949)

George S. Clason, *The Richest Man in Babylon* (New York: Penguin Books, 1955)

Said Elias Dawlabani, *MEMEnomics*: *The Next Generation Economic System* (New York: SelectBooks, Inc. 2013)

Dante Alleghieri, *Dante's Inferno*, trans. Mark Musa (Bloomington Indiana University Press, 1971)

Emily Dickinson, *Selected Poems of Emily Dickinson* (New

York: Random House, 1924)

John Donne, *The Poems of John Donne*, ed. Herbert Grierson (London: Oxford University Press, 1949)

Ralph Waldo Emerson, *Selected Writings of Emerson*, ed. Donald McQuade (New York: The Modern Library, 1981)

Favorite Folktales from Around the World, ed. Jan Yolen (New York: Pantheon Books, 1986)

Rana Foroohar, *Makers and Takers: The Rise of Finance and the Fall of American Business.* (New York: Crown Business Books, 2016)

Robert Frost, *The Poems of Robert Frost* (New York: The Modern Library, 1930)

R. Buckminster Fuller, *Operating Manual for Spaceship Earth* (New York: E. P. Dutton, 1963)

Christophe Galfard, *The Universe in Your Hand: A Journey through Space, Time, and Beyond* (New York: Flatiron Books, 2016)

Bill Gates, *The Road Ahead* (New York: Penguin Books, 1993)

Nathaniel Hawthorne, *The House of the Seven Gables* (Cutchogue, New York: Buccaneer Books, 1987)

Nathaniel Hawthorne, *Tales and Sketches* (New York: The Viking Press, 1972)

Napoleon Hill, *Think and Grow Rich* (New York: Fawcett Books, 1960)

Ernest Holmes, *The Science of Mind* (New York: G.P. Putnam's Sons, 1988)

Robinson Jeffers, *Roan Stallion, Tamar, and Other Poems* (New York: Horace Liveright, 1925), p. 232

James Joyce, *Dubliners* (New York: The Viking Press, 1958)

Franz Kafka, "The Judgment," *Psychological Fiction*, ed. Morris Beja (Glenview, Illinois: Scott, Foresman & Company, 1971)

Franz Kafka, "The Metamorphosis," *Classics of Modern Fiction: Ten Short Novels*, ed. Irving Howe (New York: Harcourt Brace Jovanovich, Inc., 1980)

Robert Kiyosaki, with Sharon L. Lechter, *Rich Dad Poor Dad* (Paradise Valley, Arizona: TechPress, Inc., 1998)

Axel Leijonhufvud, *On Keynesian Economics and the Economics of Keynes: A Study in Monetary Theory* (London: Oxford University Press, 1968).

Niccolo Machiavelli, *The Prince*, trans. T. G. Bergin (New York: Appleton- Century, Crofts, 1947)

Eric Morath, "Soaring Child-Care Costs Squeeze Families," *The Wall Street Journal*, July 2-3, 2016 A3

Herman Melville, "Bartelby the Scrivener A Story of Wall Street," *Psychological Fiction*, ed. Morris Beja (Glenville, Illinois: Scott, Foresman & Company, 1971, p.235-265.

David Perkins, ed., *English Romantic Writers* (New York: Harcourt, Brace, & World, 1967.

Tom Rath, *Strengths Finder 2.0* (New York: Gallup Press, 2007)

Jeremy Rifkin, *The End of Work* (New York: G. B. Putnam's Sons, 1995).

Carlo Rovelli, *Seven Brief Lessons on Physics* (New York: Riverhead Books, 2016)

Carl Sagan, *Cosmos* (New York: Random House, 1980).

Erwin Schrodinger, *My View of the World*, (Cambridge: Cambridge University Press, 1964).

William Shakespeare, *Shakespeare: The Complete Works*, ed. G.B. Harrison (New York: Harcourt Brace and Company, 1948)

Sophocles, *Oedipus the King*, trans. David Grene, *An Anthology of Greek Dram*a, ed. C.A. Robinson, Jr. (New York: Holt, Rinehart and Winston, 1960).

Lord Alfred Tennyson, *Tennyson's Poetry* (New York: W.W.

Norton & Company, Inc., 1971)

Rob Turner, "Investors' Biggest Mistakes," _Money Magazine_, September, 1999, 77-88.

Amy Webb, "The Industrial Evolution: Get Ready to See These Go-Between Jobs Automated Out of Existence, _INC_, July/August, 2016, p. 84

Walt Whitman, _Leaves of Grass_, Version of the First (1855) Edition, section 48, lines 1262-1280, Ed. Malcolm Cowley (New York: The Viking Press, 1961), pp. 82-83

Virginia Woolf, _To the Lighthouse_, (New York: Harcourt, Brace & World, Inc., 1927)

www.ingramcontent.com/pod-product-compliance
Lightning Source LLC
LaVergne TN
LVHW051455080426
835509LV00017B/1773